Answers to Questions Asked By Muslims

by

Yousry Sidrak

Copyright © 2026 Yousry Sidrak

All rights reserved. No part of this publication may be reproduced, stored in a retrieval system, or transmitted in any form or by any means—electronic, mechanical, photocopying, recording, or otherwise—without prior written permission of the author, except for brief quotations in reviews.

Published by Yousry Sidrak

Australia

ISBN: 978-0-646-73310-4 (Paperback)

First edition

This book is intended for educational and scholarly discussion. The views expressed are those of the author.

Printed in Australia

Dedication

To my beloved wife and life partner, Irene

Foreword

Islam is in revival mode. Demographers calculate that unless current trends are disrupted, Islam will become numerically the world's number one religion by the 2070s.

Through legal and illegal immigration its devotees are increasingly present especially in Western jurisdictions. While the people of those countries kill their children through abortion, Muslims cherish theirs as a blessing from Allah and a contribution toward their achieving Islam's long-term goal of international supremacy.

The church in the West, seemingly incapable of defending its historical spiritual territory is preoccupied with adjusting to the rapid rise of woke culture, political turmoil and societal polarisations. Focussed on internal issues, Western Christian leaders have little time or inclination to respond to the encroaching existential threat posed by Islam.

In Christianity's training institutes Islam is scarcely mentioned let alone studied in detail. Time and resource are still dedicated to examining the Protestant and Catholic Reformations of five centuries ago without realising that an Islamic Reformation is occurring in our midst.

It's easier to accept unexamined Islam's oft repeated mantras that "we worship the same God" and that Islam is "a religion of peace." Christian leaders, therefore, remain untrained and inexperienced in how to respond to Islam. Our ignorance shows at the highest levels.

Fortunately, not everyone is ignorant of Islam and what happens when Islam arrives and implements its harsh, 7th century Shariah Law. Whereas in most countries which have been forced to surrender to Islamic invasion which resulted in the eventual destruction of their culture and non-Islamic religious expressions, Egypt has proven to be an exception.

Since the completion of the Arab army's invasion of Egypt in 642, a minority of Christians have managed to survive all oppression and persecution. They have maintained their allegiance to Jesus of the Bible. When these people speak the rest of us need to listen carefully because they speak from centuries of painful experience.

Muslim preachers unlike many of their Christian counterparts, are very well trained, especially in apologetics and Christian theology. They know how to confuse Christians and attract them toward Islam by asking questions which few Christians can answer.

A question often has two sides. Our politicians usually take both. Alas, the luxury of such avoidance of answering is not afforded to innocent Christians who have probably never faced questioning let alone trying to come up with answers. And as for Islam's destructive claims against Christian and Jewish beliefs, we've mostly never even read Islam's sacred texts in which its claims are securely incubated.

Like the West's political structures of liberal secular democracy, our ignorance is bliss, until it's not, which is usually too late.

Dr Yousry Sidrak of Egyptian origin has come to our rescue. His book, *Answers to Questions Asked by Muslims*, gives answers to 36 questions Muslims commonly ask Christians to undermine their confidence and destroy their faith. It is a welcome defensive weapon which needs to be added to every Christian's equipment.

Even if one is never subjected to Islamic cross examination this book alone can save us buying many other weighty tomes of Christian theology that attempt to explain the almost inexplainable. After reading them, often we remain lost and confused in an impenetrable forest of words and worse off financially.

Dr Sidrak's explanations are clear, concise and precise. He also has another advantage which few Christian theologians or preachers have. He is fluent in his mother tongue—Arabic, which is the language of the Qur'an. This is hugely important.

In Christianity the Word became flesh—Jesus (John 1:14). In Islam the Word became a book—the Quran—in Arabic (Q.4:171; 43:3). Muslims claim that the Quran in any language other than Arabic is only an interpretation as consistently accurate translation from the original heaven inspired language of Arabic is not possible. This enables them to mount arguments against Christianity while secluding their own texts from equal examination behind classic Arabic. This cannot happen with Sidrak. In supplying answers, he not only confidently refers to the Biblical languages of Hebrew, Aramaic and Koiné Greek, he uses Arabic to show the interrogator that often the answer to the question is to be found within the Quran itself. How disconcerting!

For anyone involved in ministry to Muslims this book is a long overdue necessity. And for those who long to understand almost the unfathomable of the Christian faith this book makes an invaluable contribution toward simplifying complex matters while demystifying the mysterious.

Dr Stuart Robinson

Research Fellow and Lecturer

Arthur Jeffery Centre

Melbourne School of Theology

Acknowledgment

I am grateful to all who contributed to this work. My appreciation goes to apologists Dr David Wood, of Acts17Apologetics, Sam Shamoun, of the Apologist Project, Dr. Bernie Power, of Melbourne School of Theology, Melbourne, Australia, Brother Rachid of "With All Clarity" TV program and Brother Waheed of "The Evidence" TV program. Special thanks to my wife, Irene, for her patience, understanding and encouragement throughout this work.

Contents

Dedication iii

Foreword iv

Acknowledgment vii

Introduction xii

Question 1 Where did Jesus say "I am God, worship Me?" 14

Question 2 Shouldn't Adam be greater than Jesus? 18

Question 3 Shouldn't Melchizedec be greater than Jesus? 20

Question 4 If Jesus is God, how could he die? 23

Question 5 If Jesus is God, how could he address God as "The Only True God"? 27

Question 6 Didn't Jesus admit that he was not God, or even a good person? 30

Question 7 Doesn't God have many children, so what is unique about Jesus being the Son of God? 33

Question 8 All prophets were sinless, so Jesus is not unique being sinless. Isn't that true? 36

Question 9 How could God have a Son? 40

Question 10 Is Jesus God, or the Son of God? 44

Question 11 Hasn't the Bible been corrupted? 48

Question 12 One Qur'an, why four Gospels? 53

Question 13 Isn't the Bible obsolete since the Qur'an has superseded it? 57

Question 14 How could Jesus be a man of peace when he said "I came to bring a sword, not peace"? 60

Question 15 How could Jesus be God, when he was ignorant of the last Hour?..64

Question 16 Isn't discrepancy in King Ahaziah's age a proof of the Bible's corruption?...68

Question 17 How could a kind Lord call a woman "a dog"? 71

Question 18 Aren't Bible Wars even worse than Islamic Jihad?...75

Question 19 Hasn't Apostle Paul corrupted Jesus' teachings?.....79

Question 20 Wasn't Jesus helpless when he said "Of Myself, I can do nothing"?...85

Question 21 How could a loving Jesus command his enemies to be slaughtered in his presence?...89

Question 22 Isn't Trinity illogical?...92

Question 23 Isn't it true that the doctrine of Trinity is the invention of Apostle Paul?...98

Question 24 Why did Jesus command to purchase swords?........103

Question 25 How could Jesus be God when He has a God? 106

Question 26 How could Jesus be God if He prayed to God?......110

Question 27 Jesus prayed and fasted like a Muslim, so wasn't he a Muslim? 113

Question 28 Apostle Barnabas wrote "Jesus wasn't crucified", Wasn't he in agreement with the Quran?...117

Question 29 Wasn't Jesus inferior to God because he said "My Father is greater than I"?...121

Question 30 Nothing special about Jesus raising the dead, haven't other Prophets raised the dead, too? 124

Question 31 How could the Gospel be trusted if it is only a translation from Aramaic language? 127

Question 32 Aren't Christians worshippers of a weak and helpless God? 130

Question 33 Who are the Gospel writers? Aren't they anonymous? 133

Question 34 How could God foresake God? 136

Question 35 Didn't Jesus, himself, say there are many Gods? ..140

Question 36 How many Lords, you Christians have? 143

About The Author 147

Introduction

Since its rise in the seventh century A.D., Islam has engaged not only with its own beliefs and the mission of Prophet Muhammad, but also with other faiths, particularly Judaism and Christianity. This was natural, for Islam emerged in the Arabian Peninsula, where Jewish communities lived in Medina (Yathrib), close to Mecca, and where Christianity was represented across the Byzantine Empire, the Aksumite kingdom, and various regional churches.

The Qur'ān urges reflection and understanding, while the Sunnah (i.e., teachings, actions, approvals and way of life of Prophet Muhammad), highlights the virtue of sincere inquiry. From the earliest generations, Muslims recognized that questions—when asked with humility—strengthen faith and deepen comprehension of divine guidance. Many of these questions have concerned the religions mentioned in the Qur'ān, especially Christianity and Judaism.

Because much attention has focused on the origins of Christianity, the Gospel and, before all, the identity of Jesus Christ, this volume, Answers to Questions Asked by Muslims, seeks to provide clear and well-sourced responses to those questions. The answers draw on the Bible, the Qur'ān, the Sunnah (or hadith), and the interpretations of classical scholars.

The purpose of this work is to offer scholarly, reliable, and accessible explanations to common inquiries about the Christian faith, its doctrines, its Scriptures, and its understanding of the identity of Jesus Christ. It is written to promote clarity, correct misunderstandings, and build bridges of understanding between Christians and Muslims.

This book is not intended as light reading; many answers are necessarily detailed. It will be of value to Christian apologists and evangelists engaged in dialogues with Muslims, though it is hoped that all readers, including Muslims, will benefit. While no single work can address every question or replace the guidance of qualified scholars, this volume is offered as a trustworthy resource for study and conversation.

For convenience, most references are included throughout. Biblical quotations are taken from the New International Version (NIV), and Qur'anic citations follow the translation of Abdullah Yusuf Ali.

The words "God" and "Allah" are, sometimes, used interchangeably. All biblical and Qur'anic verses are *italic*.

For Muslim readers' convenience, names of biblical books are given in full, i.e., without abbreviation.

References from the Qur'an are in the form (Qur'an a:b), where "a" is Chapter, or Surah, number, and "b" is verse number.

Question 1

Since Christians worship Jesus as God, where did Jesus say, in the Bible, "I am God, worship me"

Answer

This is perhaps the most frequent question Muslims pose when engaging with Christians: "Where did Jesus say, in exact words, 'I am God, worship me'?"

Muslims know that such an explicit statement does not appear in the Bible. As a quick response to this "exact quotation" demand, one might turn the question around by asking: "I will be happy to show you where did Jesus say, 'I am God, worship me,' if you can show me where did Jesus say, in those exact words, 'I am not God, do not worship me.'"

Since no such words exist, the Qur'ānic claim that Jesus was merely a prophet is equally unsupported by "exact wording." Thus, the demand for verbatim quotations is not a serious search for truth, but rather a rhetorical device to confuse.

Once we move beyond this "exact words" criterion, a more reasonable question arises:

"Where and how did Jesus claim to be God in the Bible?"

At this point, interpretation becomes essential. The Bible records many statements and actions of Jesus that reveal divine identity—not in slogans, but in claims and attributes that, according to both the Bible and the Qur'ān, belong only to God almighty.

ANSWERS TO QUESTIONS

Claims that Belong to God Alone

1. The First and the Last

"This is what the LORD says—Israel's King and Redeemer, the LORD Almighty: I am the first and I am the last; apart from me there is no God." (Isaiah 44:6)

"He is the First and the Last, the Evident and the Hidden; and He has full knowledge of all things." (Qur'ān 57:3)

Jesus made the same claim: *"Do not be afraid. I am the First and the Last. I am the Living One; I was dead, and now look, I am alive for ever and ever!"* (Revelation 1:17–18)

2. The Forgiver of Sins

""I, even I, am he who blots out your transgressions, for my own sake, and remembers your sins no more" (Isaiah 43:25)

"...and who can forgive sins except Allah?" (Qur'ān 3:135)

Yet Jesus forgave sins: *"Son, your sins are forgiven."* The scribes rightly asked, *"Who can forgive sins but God alone?"* (Mark 2:5–12). Jesus then healed the paralytic to prove his authority to forgive sins.

3. The Final Judge

"For there I will sit to judge all the nations." (Joel 3:12; cf. Psalm 9:7–8)

"On that Day, the dominion will be Allah's: He will judge between them." (Qur'ān 22:56–57)

Jesus claimed the same role: *"When the Son of Man comes... all nations will be gathered before him, and he will separate the people one from another."* (Matthew 25:31–32; cf. John 5:29).

4. The Truth

"Into your hands I commit my spirit; deliver me, LORD, God of truth." (Psalm 31:5)

"That is because Allah is the Truth." (Qur'ān 22:6)

Jesus said: *"I am the way and the truth and the life."* (John 14:6).

5. The One Who Raises the Dead

"The LORD brings death and makes alive; he brings down to the grave and raises up." (1 Samuel 2:6)

"Allah will raise up all who are in the graves." (Qur'ān 22:7)

Jesus declared: *"The dead. will hear the voice of the Son of God... those who hear will live."* (John 5:25–29). He also said: *"I am the resurrection and the life."* (John 11:25).

6. The One Who Shares God's Glory

"I am the LORD; that is my name! I will not yield my glory to another." (Isaiah 42:8)

"Whatever is in the heavens and on earth declares the glory of Allah." (Qur'ān 57:1)

Yet Jesus prayed: *"Father, glorify me in your presence with the glory I had with you before the world began."* (John 17:5).

Additional Evidence

- Jesus is "Lord of the Sabbath" (Mark 2:28), though the Sabbath belongs to God alone (Exodus 31:13).
- Jesus claimed existence before Abraham: *"Before Abraham was born, I am."* (John 8:58), claiming for himself the name "Yahweh" that God called himself with (Exodus 3:14). He repeated the same claim in John 8:24.

ANSWERS TO QUESTIONS

- Jesus called himself both the "Root and Offspring of David" (Revelation 22:16), implying pre-existence and humanity.
- He declared himself greater than the temple (Matthew 12:6), the heir of all things (Matthew 11:27), and the one with all authority in heaven and on earth (Matthew 28:18–20).
- He taught that the Father's possessions are his (John 16:15) and demanded equal honour with the Father (John 5:21–23).
- Jesus was worshiped (Matthew 28:17; Luke 24:52; John 20:28), and he promised to be with his followers always, demonstrating omnipresence (Matthew 28:20; cf. Matthew 18:20).

So, to conclude, Jesus never needed to utter the words, "I am God, worship me." His claims, actions, and titles demonstrate, clearly, that he possesses the powers, prerogatives, and glory that belong to God alone. For this reason, the early Christians—and the Scriptures themselves—recognized that Jesus is indeed divine.

Question 2

Shouldn't Adam be greater than Jesus? Jesus had no father, but Adam had neither a father nor a mother.

Answer

Muslims who ask this question know and believe that Jesus was born of a virgin (Qur'ān 19:19). What they overlook, however, is that Adam was created, not born.

As the first human being, Adam's origin was a matter of necessity—he could not have a father or a mother. After Adam's creation, God established the natural order by which humanity would multiply: through the union of a man and a woman. This has been the universal pattern of human reproduction ever since.

When the appointed time came for Jesus to enter the world, however, God broke this natural cycle. Jesus was born of a virgin, without the involvement of a man, as affirmed by both the Bible (Luke 1:26–38) and the Qur'ān (Qur'an 19:19).

There are also deeper implications to this miracle. Anas ibn Mālik, a companion of Prophet Muhammad, reported that the Prophet said:-

"All descendants of Adam are sinners, and the best of the sinners are those who frequently repent."[1]

Since Jesus was not a descendant of Adam in the ordinary sense, both the Bible and the Qur'ān affirm that he was born sinless—unique among all who have ever lived. The Bible testifies to his

---

[1] Narrated by al-Tirmidhī and Ibn Mājah, with a strong chain of narration, Book 16, hadith 41

sinlessness (Luke 1:35; John 8:46; 1 Peter 2:22), and the Qur'ān describes him as *"a holy son"* (Qur'an 19:19).

So, to conclude, far from being lesser than Adam, Jesus's virgin birth sets him apart as utterly unique—sinless, holy, and unlike any other human being.

Question 3

Shouldn't Melchizedek be greater than Jesus, and shouldn't he be worshipped, since he has no father or mother, and without beginning of days or end of life, while Jesus has a beginning of days, and has a mother?

"This Melchizedek was king of Salem and priest of God Most High. He met Abraham returning from the defeat of the kings and blessed him, 2 and Abraham gave him a tenth of everything. First, the name Melchizedek means 'king of righteousness'; then also, 'king of Salem' means 'king of peace.' 3 Without father or mother, without genealogy, without beginning of days or end of life, resembling the Son of God, he remains a priest forever. 4 Just think how great he was: Even the patriarch Abraham gave him a tenth of the plunder!" (Hebrews 7:1–4)

Answer

First, let us establish the fact that Jesus left no doubt about his divinity. In one of his dialogues with the Jews, he made an astounding claim:

"Your Father Abraham rejoiced at the thought of seeing my day; he saw it and was glad." "You are not yet fifty years old," they said to him, "and you have seen Abraham!" "Very truly I tell you," Jesus answered, "before Abraham was born, I am!" (John 8:56–58)

The Jews understood him clearly: Jesus was claiming eternal existence and divine identity. That is why they tried to stone him.

Now, regarding Melchizedek: the first mention is in Genesis 14:17–20, where he appears as king of Salem and priest of God Most High. He blesses Abraham, who in turn gives him a tenth of the spoils. His priesthood is unique—not Aaronic, not based on animal sacrifices, but marked by bread and wine. This points forward to Christ, who also offered bread and wine as signs of his body and blood (Matthew 26:26–28).

No wonder, then, that Psalm 110 prophesies:

"The LORD has sworn and will not change his mind: 'You are a priest forever, in the order of Melchizedek.'" (Ps 110:4)

The psalmist reveals that Melchizedek's priesthood foreshadows Christ's eternal priesthood.

The book of Hebrews develops this: Melchizedek's priesthood is greater than the Levitical priesthood, since Abraham—the ancestor of Levi and Aaron—gave tithes to him and received his blessing (Hebrew 7:1–10). As the text explains, "the lesser is blessed by the greater" (v. 7).

But notice: the passage does not claim Melchizedek was divine. Rather, his genealogy is deliberately omitted in Scripture so that his priesthood might resemble the eternal priesthood of the Son of God. The point is typological, not literal.

Jesus, unlike Melchizedek, is not merely a type or shadow. He is the eternal Son of God, who truly lives forever and intercedes at the right hand of the Father (Psalms 110:1; Hebrew 7:25). His priesthood, in the order of Melchizedek, has no beginning and no end—not because of silence about his parents, but because he is eternal.

Therefore:

- Melchizedek was a historical king and priest, mentioned in Scripture as a symbol.
- His priesthood points beyond himself to Christ.
- The eternity spoken of in Hebrews belongs not to the man

Melchizedek, but to the priesthood he represents—fulfilled perfectly in Jesus Christ.

So, to conclude, Christians do not worship Melchizedek because Scripture never presents him as divine. Instead, he is a prophetic figure pointing to the One who truly is divine—the Lord Jesus Christ, whose eternal priesthood surpasses all others.

ANSWERS TO QUESTIONS

Question 4

If Jesus is God, how could He die?

Answer

To address this question, we must first clarify the Christian understanding of the deity of Jesus.

The Apostle John writes:

"In the beginning was the Word, and the Word was with God, and the Word was God. ... Through him all things were made."

(John 1:1–3)

Here we see that the Word (Logos) is eternal, distinct from God the Father, and yet fully divine. Verse 14 adds:

"The Word became flesh and made his dwelling among us. We have seen his glory, the glory of the one and only Son, who came from the Father, full of grace and truth."

Thus, the eternal Word of God entered human history, taking on human nature. Paul confirms this in Philippians 2:5–11, where Christ, *"being in very nature God,"* humbled Himself, took the form of a servant, and became obedient even to death on a cross.

Muslims' Objection

Muslims often argue:

"If God enters creation, He becomes dependent. And if God is dependent, He is unworthy of worship."

However, according to authentic hadith, Allah himself "descends" into creation:

"*Our Lord, the Blessed and Exalted, descends every night to the sky of this world when the last third of the night remains...*"[1]

Since time zones differ, this would mean Allah remains within creation for extended periods every night.

The Qur'an also records Allah speaking from within creation, in the account of the burning bush:

"*When he came to it, he was called from the right side of the valley, in the blessed spot, from the tree...*" (Qur'an 28:29–30)

Clearly, Islam itself affirms that God can manifest himself within creation.

At this point, Muslims often respond:

"Yes, Allah can enter creation, but He cannot die."

Muslims believe the Qur'an is the eternal, uncreated Word of Allah. Yet, in physical form, as paper and ink, it can be burned, destroyed, or desecrated. To explain this, Muslims argue that the Qur'an has two natures: one eternal and uncreated, and another physical and perishable.[2,3]

This shows that in Islamic thought, something eternal can enter creation in a material form and be destroyed without compromising its eternal nature.

Similarly, Christian theology teaches that the eternal Son of God took on human nature and entered creation. His divine nature remained eternal and indestructible, but His human nature was

---

[1] Sahih Muslim, Book of Prayer, Hadith number 758B
[2] Wolfson, Harry "*The Philosophy of the Kalam*," Harvard University Press, 1976
[3] al-Nawawi, Introduction of Sharh Sahih Muslim, under "*The Creed of Ahl al-Sunnah regarding the Speech of Allah,*" Dar Ihya al-Turath, vol. 1, p. 24-26

subject to death. Through His death, He accomplished salvation for all who believe.

A Striking Parallel

Prophet Muhammad himself taught that the Qur'an will appear on the Day of Resurrection in human form:

"The Qur'an will come on the Day of Resurrection like a pale man and will say: I am the one that kept you awake at night and made you thirsty during the day."[1]

If Muslims can accept that Allah's eternal Word may appear as a book, be subject to destruction, and even take on human form, then it should not seem illogical that God's eternal Word became flesh in Jesus Christ and died on the cross.

The Real Issue

The problem is not logical but theological. Islam cannot accept the idea of a loving God who would sacrifice Himself for humanity. In the Qur'an, Allah is a master, and people are merely His slaves:

"*There is none in the heavens and the earth but comes to the Most Merciful as a slave.*"   (Qur'an 19:93)

A master does not die for his slaves. But the God of the Bible is both just and loving. Paul writes:

"*You see, at just the right time, when we were still powerless, Christ died for the ungodly. Very rarely will anyone die for a righteous person, though for a good person, someone might possibly dare to die. But God demonstrates his own love for us in this: While we were still sinners, Christ died for us.*"   (Romans 5:6–8)

---

[1] Musnad Ahmad, Hadith number 3:352

So, to conclude, It is not impossible for God to enter creation. In fact, this is the heart of the gospel: the eternal Son of God took on flesh, entered creation, and died—not because He was weak, but because He loved us.

Question 5

How could Jesus be God if he clearly addressed the Father as "the only true God" in John 17:3?

"After Jesus said this, he looked toward heaven and prayed:

'Father, the hour has come. Glorify your Son, that your Son may glorify you. For you granted him authority over all people that he might give eternal life to all those you have given him. Now this is eternal life: that they know you, the only true God, and Jesus Christ, whom you have sent. I have brought you glory on earth by finishing the work you gave me to do. And now, Father, glorify me in your presence with the glory I had with you before the world began.'" (John 17:1–5)

Answer

The very passage Muslims point to as a challenge is, in fact, one of the strongest affirmations of Jesus' glory. John 17 records Jesus' "High Priestly Prayer," just before his arrest and crucifixion.

Let's examine the text step by step:

1. Jesus calls God his Father.

"Glorify your Son, that your Son may glorify you."

When Jesus called God his Father, the Jews understood this as a claim to equality with God in His divine nature:

"My Father is working until now, and I am working. This was why the Jews were seeking all the more to kill him ... he was even calling God his own Father, making himself equal with God." (John 5:17–18; Matt 26:63–66)

2. Jesus claims authority to give eternal life.

"...that he might give eternal life to all those you have given him."

Who grants eternal life? In John 10:27–28, Jesus says plainly:

"I give them eternal life, and they shall never perish."

And in John 5:21, Jesus adds:-

"For just as the Father raises the dead and gives them life, even so the Son gives life to whom he is pleased to give it."

Only God can give eternal life—yet Jesus claims this authority.

3. Jesus shares mutual glory and honour with the Father.

"Glorify your Son, that your Son may glorify you." (John 17:2)

This reciprocal glorification echoes John 5:22–23:

"The Father judges no one, but has entrusted all judgment to the Son, that all may honour the Son just as they honour the Father."

To honour Jesus, "just as" the Father is to acknowledge his deity.

But what about "the only true God?"

In verse 3, Jesus defines eternal life:

"...that they know you, the only true God, and Jesus Christ, whom you have sent."

Eternal life is not gained by knowing the Father alone but by knowing both the Father and the Son. John 1:18 explains why:

"No one has ever seen God, but the one and only Son, who is himself God and is in closest relationship with the Father, has made him known."

Jesus is not excluding himself from deity; rather, he reveals the Father as the Son who is himself God in divine nature.

Parallel passages confirm this.

Revelation 22:3 speaks of *"the throne of God and of the Lamb"*—one throne, shared by both.

Jude 24-25 praises *"the only God our Savior ... through Jesus Christ our Lord."*

Titus 2:13–14 calls Jesus *"our great God and Savior."* Thus, Scriptures consistently call Jesus both Lord and God.

So, to conclude, John 17:1–3 affirms both the oneness of God and the deity of Christ. The conjunction *"and"* does not separate Jesus from the Godhead, any more than it separates "God and the Lamb" in Revelation 22:3.

Far from denying Christ's divinity, this passage reveals that eternal life requires knowing the Father and the Son—because the Son shares the very glory of God the Father "the glory [he] had… before the world began."

Question 6

How could Jesus be God when He, himself, denied being God—or even being a good person—in Matthew 19:16–22?

"Just then, a man came up to Jesus and asked, 'Good teacher, what good thing must I do to get eternal life?' 'Why do you ask me about what is good?' Jesus replied. 'There is only One who is good. If you want to enter life, keep the commandments.' ...

Jesus answered, 'If you want to be perfect, go, sell your possessions and give to the poor, and you will have treasure in heaven. Then come, follow me.' When the young man heard this, he went away sad, because he had great wealth."

(Matthew 19:16–22; Mark 10:17–22)

Answer

Did Jesus deny His goodness—or His deity—in this passage? The answer is no.

1. The Qur'an Affirms Jesus' Goodness and Sinlessness

The Qur'an itself upholds Jesus' purity and righteousness. He is called:

- *"Honoured in this world and the hereafter"* (Qur'an 3:45)
- *"Pure"* and *"sinless"* (Qur'an 19:19)

Additionally, the Hadith declares that only Jesus was protected from Satan at birth:

"Every child is touched by Satan at birth, except Mary and her son."[1]

---

[1] Sahih al-Bukhari, Hadith number 3431

Thus, to deny Jesus' goodness would contradict Islam's own sources.

2. The Gospels Consistently Affirm Jesus' Sinlessness and Goodness

- *"You are to give him the name Jesus, because he will save his people from their sins."* (Matthew 1:21)
- Before his conception, the angel Gabriel told his mother of his sinlessness:- *"The Holy Spirit will come on you, and the power of the Most High will overshadow you. So the holy one to be born will be called the Son of God"* (Luke 1:35)
- *"Take heart, son; your sins are forgiven."* (Matthew 9:2)
- *"Can any of you prove me guilty of sin?"* (John 8:46)
- *"I am the good shepherd."* (John 10:11)

Clearly, Jesus did not deny His goodness. Instead, He challenged the man to consider what his words really meant.

3. The Meaning of Jesus' Response

In Jewish understanding, only God is truly good.

Goodness is not a relative human standard—it is God's very nature (Genesis 1:31; Psalms 100:5; and 119:68).

So when the man called Jesus "Good Teacher," Jesus responded:- "Why do you call me good? No one is good but God."

This was not a denial of goodness but a test of the man's understanding:

- If Jesus is good, then the man is implicitly recognizing Jesus' divinity.
- If the man does not believe Jesus is God, then calling Him "good" is meaningless flattery.

Jesus was leading the man to confront the implications of his own words.

4. **The Real Problem: Divided Allegiance**

The rich young ruler claimed to have kept the commandments, yet he walked away sad. Why?

Because he failed the first and greatest commandment—to love God above all else (Matthew 22:37-38).

His wealth mattered more to him than God. Jesus revealed that true goodness flows not from human effort but from God Himself. To be truly good is to follow Christ and place God above all possessions.

5. **The Logic Summarized**

- Jesus affirms that only God is good.
- Jesus claims goodness (John 10:11) and sinlessness (John 8:46 and others).
- Therefore, Jesus is implicitly claiming to be God.

So, to conclude, far from denying His divinity, Jesus used this encounter to reveal it.

The man sought rules for eternal life; Jesus offered Himself:

"Come, follow Me."

That invitation is the ultimate declaration of both His goodness and deity.

The story of the rich young ruler fits perfectly within Matthew's broader narrative, which consistently unveils Jesus as the eternal, divine Son of God.

Question 7

What is so special about Jesus being called "The Son of God". The Bible calls others sons of God, too. Christians are sons of God (John 1:12), and even Adam is called the son of God (Luke 3:38).

Answer

Muslims often fail to distinguish between the different types of "sonship" described in the Bible. Let us first explain these types, and then show why Jesus' sonship is utterly unique.

The Bible presents three categories of sonship:

1. Sonship by creation – Adam is called "the son of God" because he was directly created by God (Luke 3:38).
2. Sonship by adoption – All who believe in Christ are graciously adopted into God's family:

"Yet to all who did receive him, to those who believed in his name, he gave the right to become children of God—children born not of natural descent, nor of human decision or a husband's will, but born of God." (John 1:12–13)

3. Unique, divine sonship – This is true of Jesus Christ alone. When Jesus claimed to be the Son of God, the Jewish leaders understood this as a claim to equality with God in divine nature:

"He was even calling God his own Father, making himself equal with God." (John 5:18)

"I and the Father are one." ... *"We are not stoning you for any good work,"* they replied, *"but for blasphemy, because you, a mere man, claim to be God."* (John 10:30–33)

No Christian believer is ever stoned for calling himself a child of God. But Jesus was condemned to death for precisely this claim—

because his sonship was unique, not by creation or adoption, but by nature.

When questioned by the high priest:

"Are you the Messiah, the Son of the Blessed One?". "I am," said Jesus. "And you will see the Son of Man sitting at the right hand of the Mighty One and coming on the clouds of heaven."

The high priest tore his clothes. "You have heard the blasphemy… He is worthy of death." (Mark 14:61–64)

Here, Jesus not only affirmed his divine sonship but also identified himself with the "Son of Man" mentioned in Daniel 7—a heavenly figure who receives worship and eternal authority from the "Ancient of Days":

"He was given authority, glory and sovereign power; all nations and peoples of every language worshiped him. His dominion is an everlasting dominion." (Daniel 7:14)

The high priest and scribes understood exactly what Jesus was claiming: divine authority, heavenly enthronement, and universal worship. That is why the high priest tore his garments in outrage.

One can clearly see the contrast with the earthly high priest. In Leviticus 16, the earthly high priest could enter the Most Holy Place only once a year, and even then under the fear of death. By contrast, Jesus entered not the earthly sanctuary, but the heavenly one:

"We have this hope as an anchor for the soul, firm and secure. It enters the inner sanctuary behind the curtain, where our forerunner, Jesus, has entered on our behalf. He has become a high priest forever…" (Hebrews 6:19–20).

Thus Jesus' claim was staggering: the Son of Man would not only sit at God's right hand but would one day judge even the high priest himself.

There are indeed many ways the Bible speaks of being "sons of God," but Jesus' sonship is utterly unique.

- Adam is a son by creation.
- Believers are sons by adoption.
- Jesus alone is Son by nature, equal with the Father, worthy of worship, and enthroned in heaven.

This is why his claim provoked charges of blasphemy and led to his crucifixion. Jesus' sonship is not ordinary—it is divine.

So, to conclude, the sonship that Jesus claimed to God is, indeed, so unique that it is not shared by anyone else who ever walked the earth.

Question 8

Why would Jesus be special in his sinlessness? After all, all prophets were sinless.

Answer

Certain Muslim scholars maintain that prophets were preserved from sin (Isma'h, عِصْمَة, an Arabic word that means preserved from sinning). They argue that since Allah guides them, they cannot go astray. For instance:

- "All the prophets were decidedly guided by Allah, and whom Allah guides, there is none that can lead him astray." (Qur'an 39:37). Since every sin is regarded as misguidance, this reasoning concludes that prophets must be sinless.
- The Qur'an says:

"And whoever obeys Allah and the Apostle—these are with those upon whom Allah has bestowed favours of the prophets, the truthful, the martyrs and the righteous" (Qur'an 4:69).

The argument follows: if the prophets sinned, they would have gone astray and thus would not be recipients of Allah's favour.

Similarly, Allamah Sayyid M.H. Tabataba'i insists that if prophets committed error, were misled, or distorted revelation, God's program of guidance would be undermined.[1]

Despite these claims, both the Qur'an and hadith clearly attribute sins and errors to the prophets. A few examples:

1. Adam and Eve

---

[1] Tabataba'i, S., "The Qur'an in Islam: Its Impact and Influence on the Life of Muslims," London: Zahra Publications, p. 80, 1987.

ANSWERS TO QUESTIONS

- *"They said: 'Our Lord! We have wronged ourselves. If You forgive us not... we shall certainly be of the losers'"* (Qur'an 7:23).
- *"Thus did Adam disobey his Lord, and he went astray"* (Qur'an 20:121).

2. Prophet Noah

- *"Unless You forgive me and have mercy on me, I would indeed be one of the losers"* (Qur'an 11:47).
- *"My Lord! Forgive me, and my parents, and... all the believing men and women"* (Qur'an 71:28).

3. Prophet Abraham

- In his youth, he worshipped the star, moon, and sun (Qur'an 6:76–79), contradicting the command to worship none but Allah (Qur'an 2:83; 11:2; 12:40; etc.).
- *"And Who, I hope, will forgive me my faults on the Day of Recompense"* (Qur'an 26:82).

4. Prophet Moses

- *"He said: 'My Lord! Verily, I have wronged myself, so forgive me'"* (Qur'an 28:16).

5. Prophet Aaron

- Moses prays: *"O my Lord! Forgive me and my brother"* (Qur'an 7:151).

6. Prophet David

- *"And Dawud... sought forgiveness of his Lord"* (Qur'an 38:24).

7. Prophet Solomon

- "*My Lord! Forgive me and bestow upon me a kingdom…*" (Qur'an 38:35).

8. Prophet Jonah
  - "*Truly, I have been of the wrongdoers*" (Qur'an 21:87).
  - He is called *muleem* (blameworthy) in Qur'an 37:142—the same word used of Pharaoh (Qur'an 51:40).

9. Prophet Muhammad
  - "*Seek the forgiveness of Allah*" (Qur'an 4:106).
  - "*Ask forgiveness for your sin (dhanbik)*" (Qur'an 40:55).
  - "*That Allah may forgive you your past and future sin (dhanbik)*" (Qur'an 48:2).

Notably, the same phrase *astaghfiri li dhanbik* ("ask forgiveness for your sin") is used of Zulaykah, the wife of Potiphar, when she tried to seduce Joseph (Qur'an 12:29).

The hadith also depicts prophets confessing sins:

- On the Day of Judgement, Adam, Noah, Abraham, and Moses each refuse to intercede because of their sins.
  - Adam: disobeying God's command.
  - Noah: invoking against his people.
  - Abraham: telling "three lies."
  - Moses: killing a man unjustly.
- Only Jesus does not mention any sin. Instead, he simply declines to intercede.
- Finally, Prophet Muhammad intercedes, though the hadith

acknowledges that Allah had forgiven his "early and late sins"[1]

So, to conclude, the Qur'an and Hadith both affirm that prophets sinned and sought forgiveness—except Jesus, of whom neither the Qur'an nor the Hadith records any sin. The claim that all prophets were sinless cannot be sustained. Jesus's sinlessness, therefore, remains unique, distinguishing him from every other prophet.

---

[1] Sahih al-Bukhari, Numbers 6:236; 9:532, 601; 6:3; 8:570; 9:507

Question 9

According to the Qur'an 9:30:

"The Jews call 'Uzair a son of Allah, and the Christians call Christ the son of Allah. That is a saying from their mouths; in this they but imitate what the unbelievers of old used to say. Allah's curse be on them: how they are deluded away from the Truth."

If the Qur'an says Christians call Christ, the son of Mary, the "son of Allah," how could Allah have a son?

Answer

The Qur'an denies, in the strongest terms, that Allah could have a son:

"Say: He is Allah, the One and Only; Allah, the Eternal, Absolute; He begets not, nor is He begotten; And there is none like unto Him." (Qur'an 112:1–4)

Similar rejections appear elsewhere (Qur'an 4:171; 6:101; 19:88–92; 43:81).

Yet what the Qur'an denies here is precisely what Jews and Christians also deny: God is not begotten, physically born, nor does He Himself beget anyone.

The Qur'an itself defines this "begetting" in physical terms:

"To Him is due the primal origin of the heavens and the earth: How can He have a son وَلَد when He has no consort?"

(Qur'an 6:101)

Here, "son" is understood as one physically produced by union with a consort. Christians do not claim such a thing.

There are two different Arabic words that are translated as "Son" in the Qur'an, and let us have in mind that the Qur'an was revealed in Arabic.

- Walad وَلَد — always used when the Qur'an denies that God could have a son. This word refers to a child physically begotten.
- Ibn اِبن — used to accuse Christians calling Jesus "Son of God" (Qur'an 9:30). Ibn has a wider sense, including "belonging to."

An example of this broader sense appears in Qur'an 2:215:

"Whatever you spend is for parents, kindred, orphans, the needy, and the ibn al-sabeel (wayfarer)."

Here, *ibn al-sabeel* literally means "son of the road," i.e., a traveler who belongs to the road, not someone physically born of it.

Thus, while Christians affirm Jesus as the "Son of God" (*ibn Allah*), they mean it in the sense of His unique belonging to God, not in the Qur'an's sense of *walad* (a physically begotten child).

The Bible, however, consistently presents Jesus as God's Son in a unique, eternal, and divine sense:

1. Conceived by the Holy Spirit (Luke 1:35).
2. Shares the Father's divine nature (John 10:30; 14:11; Colossians 1:19).
3. Originates from heaven (John 6:38, 62; 8:23).
4. Eternal existence with the Father (John 1:1–3; Col. 1:15–20; John 17:5, 24).
5. Mutual knowledge with the Father (John 10:15).
6. In the bosom of the Father (John 1:18).
7. Sent by the Father (John 5:30; and many other verses).
8. The Father testifies of him (John 5:37; 8:18).
9. Receives teaching and authority from the Father (John 7:16;

5:19–23).
10. Reveals the Father (Matt. 11:27; John 1:18).
11. Perfect obedience to the Father (John 6:35–38).
12. Will return in the Father's glory (Mark 8:38).
13. Declared by the Father to be His Son (Matt. 3:17; 17:5).
14. Returns to the Father (John 16:28).
15. Reflects the Father's character (John 14:8 9).

Importantly, this sonship is not metaphorical. The Jews sought to kill Jesus because He claimed to be "the Son of God" (John 5:18; 10:30), and His final sentence of death was for declaring, *"I am the Son of God"* (Matt. 26:63–66).

Even the Qur'an itself portrays Jesus as belonging to God in a way that is absolutely unique:

1. The Word of God — Jesus alone is called "the Word of Allah" (Qur'an 3:45; 4:171). At the resurrection, people will address Him: *"O Jesus, Word of God and a Spirit from Him, intercede for us"*[1]
2. Raised alive to God — *"O Jesus! I will take you and raise you to Myself"* (Qur'an 3:55). Only Jesus is alive in heaven today.
3. Holy from birth — *"I give you glad tidings of a holy son"* (Qur'an 19:19). In Islam, holiness is a divine attribute.
4. Performs divine acts of creation and life-giving — Jesus gives sight to those born blind, heals lepers, raises the dead, and creates life by breathing into clay birds (Qur'an 3:49). These are powers of God alone (Qur'an 22:7).

So, to conclude, the Qur'an rejects the idea of God having a *walad* (a son through physical generation). Christians equally reject this. But when Christians confess Jesus as the "Son of God," they use the

---

[1] Sahih Bukhari, Number 3340

word *ibn* — the one who uniquely belongs to God in His nature, origin, authority, and mission.

Ironically, the Qur'an itself attributes to Jesus qualities and titles that confirm this unique sonship: He is God's Word, His Spirit, His Holy One, raised alive to Him, and the giver of life.

Question 10

Is Jesus God or the Son of God?

Muslims sometimes ask: "Why do Christians call Jesus God as well as the Son of God?". Surely Jesus couldn't be God and the Son of God at the same time."

Answer

The answer is: Both. Jesus is both God and the Son of God, but how?

Before turning to the Bible, let us note that according to the Qur'an itself, Jesus shares far more in common with God than Prophet Muhammad does:

The Qur'an on	... God	& Jesus	Muhammad
creates	35:3 ✓	3:49 ✓	could ✗
heals	26:80 ✓	5:110 ✓	do ✗
raises dead	22:6 ✓	3:49 ✓	no ✗
fed hungry	6:14 ✓	5:112 ✓	miracles ✗
changed law	2:106 ✓	3:50 ✓	NO 10:15 ✗
knows hidden things	5:109 ✓	3:49 ✓	NO 6:50 ✗
knows last hour	7:187 ✓	43:61 ✓	NO 72:25 ✗
Holy / sinless	59:23 ✓	19:19 ✓	NO 4:106 ✗
is in heaven	2:255 ✓	3:55 ✓	NO 46:9 ✗

So, even by Qur'anic standards, Jesus' uniqueness far exceeds Prophet Muhammad's.

So, is Jesus "God" or "the Son of God"?

The correct answer is: He is both.

A simple analogy helps. Every person is "human" by nature—we all share the same human essence. Yet each person also has a unique personal identity that no one else shares.

- Nature/essence: What we are (human, or in Jesus' case, divine).
- Person/identity: Who we *are* as individuals (John, Mary, or Jesus the Son of God).

Thus, Jesus is "God" because He shares the divine nature with the Father and the Holy Spirit. He is also "the Son of God" because that is His unique, eternal identity within the Trinity.

But Why Do Christians Say Jesus Is God?

Christians affirm Jesus' deity because He has attributes, powers, and honours that belong to God alone.

(a) **Jesus is Creator**
- Qur'an: God alone is Creator (Qur'an 6:102).
- Bible: *"The LORD is the everlasting Creator"* (Isaiah 40:28).
- Qur'an: Jesus creates (Qur'an 3:49; 5:110).
- Bible: *"Through him all things were made"* (John 1:3,10; Colossians 1:16; Hebrews 1:2; 1 Corinthians 8:6).

(b) **Jesus is eternal**
- Qur'an: God is eternal (Qur'an 112:2; 2:255).
- Bible: God is "from everlasting" (Psalms 90:2).
- Jesus: came from heaven (John 6:33,38,62), was "before Abraham" (John 8:58), shared glory with the Father "before the world began" (John 17:5,24).
- Prophets foresaw His pre-existence (Micah 5:2; Provoverbs 8:23; Isaiah 6:1; John 12:41).

(c) **Jesus is holy and sinless**
- Qur'an: God is "the Holy One" (Qur'an 59:23). Jesus is called "a holy son" (Qur'an 19:19).

- Bible: God alone is holy (1 Samuel 2:2; Revelation 15:4). Yet Jesus is called "the Holy One" (Luke 1:35), "without sin" (Hebrews 4:15). Even Jesus' enemies found "no fault in him" (John 18:38).

(d) **Jesus claimed divine powers**
- Forgives sins (Mark 2:5; Luke 7:48).
- Judges all humanity (Matthew 25:31–32; John 5:29).
- His words outlast creation (Matthew 24:35).
- Speaks with divine authority: Unlike other prophets, who affirm their sayings by: "Thus says the LORD", over 200 times in the Gospel, Jesus used "Truly, I say to you".
- Gives eternal life (John 10:28).
- Demands supreme love and loyalty (Luke 14:26).

(e) **Jesus received worship**
(Matthew 14:33; 28:9,17; Luke 24:52; John 9:38).

(f) **Jesus shares God's titles**
Light (Psalm 27:1 / John 8:12), Creator (Isaiah 40:28 / Colossians 1:16), First and Last (Isaiah 48:12 / Revelation 22:13), Saviour (Isaaiah 43:3 / John 4:42), Judge (Deuteronomy 32:35 / John 5:29), and many more.

(g) **Jesus was accused of claiming to be God**
- *"He was even calling God his own Father, making himself equal with God"* (John 5:18).
- *"Because you, a mere man, claim to be God"* (John 10:33). Jesus never denied this.

(h) **Jesus accepted being called God**
- Thomas confessed: *"My Lord and my God!"* (John 20:28). Jesus affirmed, rather than rebuked Thomas.

(i) **The Gospel explicitly teaches Jesus' divinity**
- *"Christ, who is God over all"* (Romans 9:5).
- *"Your throne, O God"* (Hebrews 1:8).

- *"Our great God and Saviour, Jesus Christ"* (Titus 2:13).
- *"Jesus Christ… the true God"* (1 John 5:20).

(j) **Jesus is enthroned in heaven**

- Seated at the right hand of the Father (Ephesians 1:20; Hebrews 1:3).
- Shares the throne of God (Revelations 22:1,3).
- Worshipped as "the Lamb at the center of the throne" (Revelations 5:6–14).

So, to conclude, Jesus is both God and the Son of God?

- God by nature—sharing the divine essence with the Father and the Spirit.
- The Son of God by person—the unique eternal Son, who reveals the Father perfectly.

The Qur'an itself shows that Jesus uniquely shares in divine attributes that no other prophet, not even Prophet Muhammad, ever possessed. The Bible confirms that Jesus is Creator, eternal, holy, worshipped, and enthroned.

In short, Jesus is the Son of God—and that means He truly is God the Son.

Question 11

Hasn't the Bible, from which Christians derive their doctrines and beliefs, been corrupted? So, how could it be trusted?

Answer

Starting with the Qur'an, it never states that the Bible has been corrupted or tampered with. In fact, the Qur'an consistently affirms the Bible's authenticity.

To address this claim, we will examine the earliest and most reliable Islamic sources: the Qur'an itself, and the commentaries (tafsir) of Al-Tabari (d. 923), Al-Qurtubi (d. 1273), Ibn Kathir (d. 1373), and Al-Shārawy (d. 1998).

References for the Qur'an can be found at www.searchtruth.com, Ibn Kathir's commentary at www.qtafsir.com, and other tafsir works at www.altafsir.com.

Some Muslims believe that certain Qur'anic verses support their belief that the Torah, the Zabur (Psalms), and the Injeel (Gospel) are unreliable because they have been tampered with. However, a closer look at the Qur'an and the works of renouned Muslim scholars shows otherwise.

The Qur'an affirms the Bible as Allah's Revelation

1. The Qur'an confirms earlier Scriptures

"To you We [i.e. Allah] sent the Scripture in truth, confirming the scripture that came before it, and guarding it in safety: so judge between them by what Allah hath revealed, and follow not their vain desires, diverging from the Truth that hath come to you." (Qur'an 5:48)

Al-Tabari explained that the first reference to "Scripture" in this verse refers to the Qur'an, while the second refers to the Torah and the Gospel. According to Al-Tabari, the Qur'an confirms the Torah and Gospel as true revelations. The word "guarding" refers to Prophet Muhammad, who was entrusted to guard and affirm the truth of the previous Scriptures.

2. Belief in all revealed Scriptures is commanded

"Say: 'We believe in Allah, and the revelation given to us, and to Abraham, Ismail, Isaac, Jacob, and the Tribes, and that given to Moses and Jesus, and that given to prophets from their Lord: We make no difference between one and another of them: And we bow to Allah." (Qur'an 2:136)

Both Al-Tabari and Ibn Kathir agree: the Torah and the Gospel were divinely revealed and must be believed in by Muslims as much as the Qur'an itself.

3. The Gospel is guidance and light

"And in their footsteps We sent Jesus, son of Mary, confirming the Torah that had come before him, and We gave him the Gospel, in which was guidance and light and confirmation of the Torah that had come before it—a guidance and admonition for the pious. Let the people of the Gospel judge by what Allah has revealed therein. Whoever does not judge by what Allah has revealed—such are the rebellious." (Qur'an 5:46–47)

The Qur'an explicitly calls the Gospel "guidance and light." It does not describe it as falsehood or corruption.

4. Denial of the revealed Books is condemned

"O you who believe! Believe in Allah and His Messenger, and the Scripture which He has sent to His Messenger, and the Scripture

which He sent to those before him. Whoever denies Allah, His angels, His Books, His Messengers, and the Last Day has gone far, far astray." (Qur'an 4:136)

The Arabic expression for "gone far astray" is kafir, meaning unbeliever or infidel. In other words, anyone who denies the authenticity of Allah's revealed Books is an unbeliever.

5. The Qur'an confirms previous revelations repeatedly

The Qur'an states no fewer than 18 times that it is a confirmation (muṣaddiqan) of the Scriptures that came before it (e.g. Quran 2:41, 89, 91, 97, 101; 3:3, 50, 81; 4:47; 5:46, 48; 6:92; 10:37; 12:111; 35:31; 46:12, 30; 61:6).

In addition, the Qur'an affirms that no one can change Allah's words:

"No change can there be in the words of Allah. This is indeed the supreme victory." (Qur'an 10:64)

"The word of your Lord is fulfilled in truth and in justice. None can change His words. He is the All-Hearing, the All-Knowing." (Qur'an 6:115)

"We have, without doubt, sent down the Message; and We will assuredly guard it (from corruption)." (Qur'an 15:9)

This promise of preservation applies to all revealed Scriptures—including the Torah, Psalms, and Gospel.

The Qur'an itself quotes from the Psalms:

"Before this, We wrote in the Psalms, after the Message (given to Moses): 'My righteous servants shall inherit the earth.'" (Qur'an 21:105)

If Allah's words cannot be changed, then the Torah, the Psalms, and the Gospel, as His revealed Books, remain preserved.

Muslims often cite Qur'an 5:13 and 2:79 to argue for corruption of the Bible.

Qur'an 5:13

"But because of their breach of their covenant, We cursed them and made their hearts hard. They change words from their proper places and forget much of what they were reminded of..."

Muslim scholars explain this verse as a distortion of interpretation, not an alteration of the text itself:

- Al-Tabari: They wrote what was not in Allah's book and falsely told the unlearned that it was from Allah.
- Al-Qurtubi: They misinterpreted Allah's words, presenting their interpretation as the true meaning.
- Al-Shārawy: They introduced sayings that were not from Allah, claiming they were divine.

Thus, this verse refers to false interpretation, not textual corruption.

Qur'an 2:79

"Woe to those who write the Book with their own hands and then say, 'This is from Allah,' to profit by it. Woe to them for what their hands have written and for the profit they gain thereby."

Again, the tafsir clarifies:

- Al-Tabari: Unlearned people wrote their own words, sold them, and falsely claimed they were from Allah.
- Ibn Kathir: People who pretended to know Allah's Book, but taught what was not in it.

- Al-Shārawy: Individuals—possibly priests—fabricated writings or issued rulings for gain, probably as amulets, but these writings never became part of the true Scriptures.

Therefore, neither verse teaches that the Torah, the Psalms, or the Gospel, were corrupted.

So, to conclude, the Torah, the Psalms and the Gospel, contained in the Bible, are divinely revealed Books from Allah. Both Prophet Muhammad and every Muslim are commanded to believe in them. The Qur'an repeatedly affirms that no one can alter Allah's words, and respected Muslim scholars confirm that verses sometimes used to claim textual corruption actually refer only to false interpretations or external writings—not to the Biblical text itself.

Professor Abdullah Saeed of Melbourne University concludes:[1]

"Since the 'authorized' scriptures of Jews and Christians remain very much today as they existed at the time of the Prophet, it is difficult to argue that the Qur'anic references to them were only to the 'pure' versions that existed at the time of Moses and Jesus. The wholesale dismissive attitude held by many Muslims in the modern period towards the scriptures of Judaism and Christianity does not seem to have the support of either the Qur'an or the major figures of tafsir."

---

[1] Saeed, A., "*The Charge of Distortion of Jewish and Christian Scriptures*," Muslim World, Fall 2002, Vol. 92, Issue 3/4, p. 419

Question 12

"We have one Qur'an.", Muslims claim. Why do Christians have four Gospels—Matthew, Mark, Luke, and John? Isn't that an indication of corruption and unnecessary repetition?

Answer

The four Gospels are not an indication of corruption, but rather of divine inspiration and completeness. Each Gospel presents Jesus Christ from a unique perspective, written for different audiences, yet all in harmony with one another.

The Gospel according to Matthew

Matthew, the tax collector mentioned in Matthew 10:3, is the author of the first Gospel. His Gospel is addressed primarily to the Jews and presents Jesus as the promised Messiah and the Lion of the tribe of Judah (Revelation 5:5; Genesis 49:10).

It begins with: *"The book of the genealogy of Jesus Christ, the son of David, the son of Abraham"* (Matthew 1:1). The emphasis on "son of David" is crucial because the Jews expected their Messiah to be a descendant of King David. Since the Messiah was also prophesied to come from the tribe of Judah, Matthew highlights this by tracing Jesus' genealogy through Abraham, Isaac, Jacob, and Judah (Matthew 1:2). Judah is singled out, while his eleven brothers are not emphasized.

Because Matthew's purpose is to demonstrate that Jesus is the Messiah foretold in the Jewish Scriptures, he frequently uses the phrase: *"All this took place to fulfill what the Lord had spoken by the prophet ..."*—a theme more prominent in Matthew than in any other Gospel.

The Gospel according to Mark

Mark, also called John Mark (Acts 12:12), was a nephew of Barnabas (Acts 15:37) and a close companion of Apostle Peter. His Gospel is directed to Christians in Rome and presents Jesus as the servant who came to serve.

The central verse of Mark's Gospel is: *"For even the Son of Man did not come to be served, but to serve, and to give his life as a ransom for many"* (Mark 10:45).

Unlike Matthew and Luke, Mark does not provide a genealogy, since a servant's lineage is irrelevant. Instead, he begins with: *"The beginning of the good news about Jesus the Messiah, the Son of God"* (Mark 1:1). Characteristically, Mark uses the phrase *"and immediately"* 43 times, reflecting the urgency and action of a servant's work.

Mark's Gospel is often called "the Gospel of action," because it emphasizes what Jesus did more than what He said.

The Gospel according to Luke

Luke, "the beloved physician" (Colossians 4:14), was a companion of Apostle Paul and also the author of the Book of Acts. His Gospel is addressed to the Greek Gentiles and presents Jesus as the Son of Man. For this reason, Luke traces Jesus' genealogy all the way back to Adam, ending with: *"... the son of Adam, the son of God"* (Luke 3:38).

Luke gives detailed accounts of Jesus' birth, His obedience to His parents, and His growth: *"And Jesus grew in wisdom and stature, and in favor with God and man"* (Luke 2:52).

Luke highlights Jesus' humanity and compassion. He records unique accounts such as:

- Jesus comforting the widow at Nain, saying, *"Do not weep"* before raising her dead son to life (Luke 7:13-15).
- His tender response to the woman with the bleeding issue: *"Daughter, your faith has made you well; go in peace"* (Luke 8:48).
- His healing of the woman crippled for eighteen years, saying, *"Woman, you are freed from your infirmity"* (Luke 13:12).

Because Luke was a physician, he included miracles of healing in his gospel more than the other three, Matthew, Mark, and John.

The Gospel according to John

The fourth Gospel was written by the apostle John, the son of Zebedee and brother of James—the disciple whom Jesus loved (John 13:23). Unlike the Synoptic Gospels (Matthew, Mark, and Luke), John's Gospel is unique.

John does not provide a human genealogy. Instead, he takes his readers back to eternity before creation: *"In the beginning was the Word, and the Word was with God, and the Word was God"* (John 1:1). And, speaking about Jesus, John writes: *"Through him all things were made; without him nothing was made that has been made. In him was life, and that life was the light of all mankind"* (John 1:3–4).

While the Synoptics, gospels according to Matthew, Mark and Luke, present Jesus as the Son of David, the Son of Abraham, and the Son of Adam, John presents Him as *"the one and only Son of God"*— the eternal Logos, the eternal Word of God.

So, to conclude, each of the four Gospels portrays Jesus Christ from a distinct perspective:

- Matthew: the promised Messiah for the Jews.

- Mark: the servant of God.
- Luke: the compassionate Son of Man.
- John: the eternal Son of God.

The four gospels are not repetitive but complementary, together giving the reader the full picture of who Jesus is. Only writers inspired by the Holy Spirit could produce such a unified and complete testimony.

ANSWERS TO QUESTIONS

Question 13

Some Muslims, when offered the Bible by Christians, refuse to accept it on the grounds that the Bible has been superseded by the Qur'an. But is this really the case?

Answer

The Qur'an repeatedly affirms that it did not come to replace or supersede the divinely inspired Scriptures revealed before it.

"It is He Who sent down to you, in truth, the Book, confirming what went before it; and He sent down the Law and the Gospel before this, as a guide to mankind, and He sent down the criterion (of judgment between right and wrong). Then those who reject Faith in the Signs of Allah will suffer the severest penalty, and Allah is Exalted in Might, Lord of Retribution." (Qur'an 3:3–4)

The phrase "confirming what went before it" translates the Arabic expression "مُصَدِّقًا لِمَا بَيْنَ يَدَيْهِ" (muṣaddiqan limā bayna yadayhi), which literally means "that which is in his hands." This indicates that the Qur'an came to confirm the Scriptures already in existence at the time of Prophet Muhammad — namely, the Gospel (Injil), the Psalms (Zubbur), and the Torah.

This same theme appears elsewhere:

"And in their footsteps We sent Jesus the son of Mary, confirming the Law that had come before him: We sent him the Gospel: therein was guidance and light, and confirmation of the Law that had come before him: a guidance and an admonition to those who fear Allah." (Qur'an 5:46–47)

Clearly, both the Gospel and the Torah were recognized as present and authoritative during Prophet Muhammad's lifetime.

Furthermore, the Qur'an records God reminding Jesus of the revelation He had given him:

"Then will Allah say: 'O Jesus, son of Mary! Recount My favor to you and to your mother. Behold! I strengthened you with the Holy Spirit, so that you spoke to the people in childhood and in maturity. Behold! I taught you the Book and Wisdom, the Law and the Gospel. And behold! you make out of clay, as it were, the figure of a bird, by My leave, and you breathe into it and it becomes a bird by My leave. And you heal those born blind, and the lepers, by My leave. And behold! you bring forth the dead by My leave. And behold! I restrained the Children of Israel from (violence to) you when you showed them the clear Signs, but the unbelievers among them said: 'This is nothing but evident magic.'" (Qur'an 5:110)

Even more striking is that many Muslims today actively search for and publish what they claim to be prophecies of Prophet Muhammad that exist in the Torah and the Gospel[1]—books they simultaneously claim were "superseded."

The extraction of those prophecies from the Bible are based on this verse:-

"Those who follow the Messenger, the unlettered Prophet, whom they find mentioned in their own scriptures—in the Law and the Gospel—he commands them what is just and forbids them what is evil; he allows them as lawful what is good and prohibits them from what is bad; he releases them from their heavy burdens and from the yokes that were upon them. So those who believe in him, honour him, help him, and follow the light which is sent down with him—it is they who will prosper." (Qur'an 7:157)

---

[1] Fathi, W. *"130 of Prophecies of the Seal of the Prophets, in the Torah, the Gospel and books of the prophecies."* Dar Al-Tawheed for Turath, Alexandria, Egypt, 2018.

In addition, the People of the Book—Jews and Christians—are explicitly commanded in the Qur'an to uphold their own Scriptures:

"Say: 'O People of the Book! You have no ground to stand upon unless you stand fast by the Law, the Gospel, and all the revelation that has come to you from your Lord.'" (Qur'an 5:68)

"Let the people of the Gospel judge by what Allah has revealed therein. If any do fail to judge by what Allah has revealed, they are (no better than) those who rebel." (Qur'an 5:47)

If the Qur'an had truly superseded the Gospel and the Torah, the People of the Book would have been told to abandon their Scriptures and follow only the Qur'an. Instead, they are commanded to stand fast by the revelations already given to them.

So, to conclude, the Qur'an does not claim to supersede the Gospel or the Torah. On the contrary, it:

- Affirms their divine origin and authority.
- Recognizes their existence during the time of Prophet Muhammad.
- Muslims today claim that they contain prophecies of Prophet Muhammad.
- Commands Jews and Christians to uphold their own Scriptures.

So, the assertion that the Bible was superseded by the Qur'an is inconsistent with the Qur'an itself.

Question 14

How could Jesus be a man of peace—who came to bring peace—when He Himself denied that?

"I did not come to bring peace, but a sword." (Matthew 10:34–36)

Answer

The words of Jesus in Matthew 10:34–36 have long prompted careful theological reflection:

"Do not think that I came to bring peace to the earth; I did not come to bring peace, but a sword. For I came to set a man against his father, a daughter against her mother, a daughter-in-law against her mother-in-law, and a man's enemies will be the members of his own household." (Matthew 10:34–36)

At first reading, this seems to clash with the broader portrait of Jesus in Scripture. The Messiah is prophetically named the Prince of Peace (Isaiah 9:6). He commands His followers to love their enemies (Matthew 5:44; Luke 6:27–28), to practice forgiveness (Matthew 6:14–15; 18:21–22; Mark 11:25; Luke 6:37), and to reject retaliation (Matthew 5:38–39; Luke 6:27–29). In Gethsemane He even restrains Peter, saying:

"Put your sword back in its place, for all who draw the sword will die by the sword." (Matthew 26:52)

How, then, should we understand His statement, "I did not come to bring peace, but a sword"?

Understanding Matthew 10 in Context

The surrounding context is crucial. In Matthew 10, Jesus is sending out the twelve apostles to announce the nearness of the Kingdom of Heaven (vv. 5–7) and to perform acts of healing and deliverance (v.

8). Along with these instructions, He warns them that opposition, hostility, and persecution will accompany their mission (vv. 16–23).

Against this background, the "sword" clearly functions as a metaphor. It does not refer to physical violence or armed conflict. Instead, it represents the relational and social division that inevitably follows differing responses to Jesus' message. Even families—normally the closest human bonds—may be split over loyalty to Him.

Luke's parallel account makes this explicit:

"Do you think I came to bring peace on earth? No, I tell you, but division." (Luke 12:51)

The emphasis is on the division produced by truth, not on the promotion of violence.

Echoes of the Prophets

Jesus' quotation in Luke 35–36 is drawn from Micah 7:6, where the prophet laments the collapse of moral integrity within the household:

"For a son dishonours his father, a daughter rises up against her mother… a man's enemies are the members of his own household."

By invoking Micah, Jesus places His ministry squarely within the prophetic tradition. Just as Israel's prophets stirred controversy when calling the nation back to covenant faithfulness, Jesus' summons to wholehearted discipleship exposes the spiritual divide between belief and unbelief, truth and deception.

Theological Meaning of the "Sword"

The division Jesus describes is rooted in the exclusive nature of His claims. Paul conveys the same principle in 2 Corinthians 6:14–16, contrasting light with darkness, righteousness with lawlessness,

Christ with Belial, and believer with unbeliever. Jesus likewise teaches: *"No one can serve two masters."* (Matthew 6:24)

Following Christ requires a loyalty that surpasses every other allegiance. The "sword," then, symbolizes the cost of discipleship—the inevitable separation that occurs when the claims of Christ confront the values of the world.

Confirmed by History and Experience

History bears out Jesus' prediction.

- The earliest Christians encountered severe opposition from within Jewish communities (Acts 13:45; 17:5).
- Gentile believers frequently faced social exclusion and hostility (1 Peter 4:3–4).

This dynamic continues today. A well-known example is Dr Nabeel Qureshi (1983–2017), a Muslim who became a Christian and later wrote that his conversion was "the most difficult decision of my life," because it cost him deeply in terms of family and community.[1] His story captures exactly the kind of division Jesus foresaw.

Even in cultures shaped by Christian influence, those who take Jesus' teachings seriously often meet resistance, misunderstanding, or marginalization. The world resists the transforming claims of the Gospel, and Jesus warns His followers not to expect universal acceptance.

So, to conclude, the "sword" of Matthew 10:34–36 is not a call to violence, but a vivid metaphor for the division that accompanies the arrival of God's truth. Jesus does not delight in conflict; rather,

---

[1] Smith, S. "The Christian Post," 2016

conflict arises because the Gospel exposes the false peace offered by the world.

Paradoxically, this text does not undermine Jesus' title as "Prince of Peace." Instead, it clarifies it:

- Through the cross, Christ brings peace with God (Romans 5:1; Colossians 1:20).
- Yet His message also divides humanity according to how individuals respond to Him.

Peace with God often results in conflict with the world (John 15:18–19).

Ultimately, the only lasting and authentic peace—redeeming, eternal, and unshakable—is found in Christ Himself.

Question 15

How could Jesus be the all-knowing, omniscient God when He showed ignorance of the last day in Mark 13:32? Jesus said:

"But about that day or hour no one knows, not even the angels in heaven, nor the Son, but only the Father"

Answer

Let us begin by quoting the Qur'an:

"And [He will make him] a messenger to the Children of Israel, [who will say], 'Indeed I have come to you with a sign from your Lord: I will create for you out of clay, as it were, the form of a bird, then I will breathe into it, and it will become a bird by Allah's leave. I will heal the blind and the leper, and I will give life to the dead— by Allah's leave. And I will inform you of what you eat and what you store in your houses. Surely in that is a sign for you, if you are indeed believers.'" (Qur'an 3:49)

Notice that when Jesus declared His knowledge of what people ate and stored in their houses—knowledge not previously revealed to Him—the phrase "by Allah's leave" is not added. This highlights a unique aspect of Jesus' knowledge.

Moreover, and according to Qur'an 43:61, the return of Jesus is the sign for the coming of the last hour of judgement:

"And (Jesus) shall be a Sign (for the coming of) the Hour (of Judgment): therefore, have no doubt about the (Hour), but follow you Me: this is a Straight Way."

We will approach this issue in two steps:

- Did Jesus demonstrate omniscience in the Gospels?

- If so, how should we understand Mark 13:32?

Jesus' Omniscience in the Gospels

There is abundant evidence in the four Gospels that Jesus possessed supernatural knowledge. A few examples illustrate this:

- Prediction of His death and resurrection: Jesus told His disciples in detail what would happen to Him in Jerusalem—His arrest, trial, mockery, death, and resurrection on the third day (Mark 10:32–34).
- Knowledge of the temple tax coin: Jesus instructed Peter to cast a line into the sea and retrieve a coin from the mouth of the first fish caught, sufficient to pay the tax for both (Matt 17:24–27).
- The donkey for His triumphal entry: Before entering Jerusalem, Jesus described exactly where His disciples would find a donkey, and what response to give if questioned (Matt 21:1–3).
- Identification of His betrayer: Jesus revealed who among the disciples would hand Him over (Matt 26:20–25).
- Knowledge of inner thoughts: Jesus perceived people's unspoken thoughts and motives (Luke 5:22–26).
- Recognition of Nathanael: Jesus knew Nathanael before meeting him, astonishing Nathanael with His knowledge (John 1:47–49).
- The Samaritan woman: Jesus revealed intimate details of the woman's life at the well, which only she could have known (John 4:16–18).
- Death of Lazarus: Jesus knew Lazarus had died while He was still a four-day journey away (John 11:14–16).
- Raising Lazarus: Jesus foretold Lazarus's resurrection and then raised him (John 11:21–44).

These accounts, and many others, demonstrate that Jesus' knowledge far exceeded normal human limitations.

Understanding Mark 13:32

Mark 13:32–33 records Jesus saying:

"Heaven and earth will pass away, but my words will never pass away. But about that day or hour no one knows, not even the angels in heaven, nor the Son, but only the Father."

First, note the remarkable claim: Jesus places His words on the same level as eternal truth— "Heaven and earth will pass away, but my words will never pass away." He is already exalted above the angels (Hebrews 1:1–4).

How then should we interpret His statement that the Son does not know the day or hour?

St. Augustine of Hippo explained:

"According to the form of God, everything that the Father has belongs to the Son: for '*All things that are mine are yours, and yours are mine*' (John 17:10). According to the form of a servant, however, his teaching is not His own but belongs to the One who sent him. Hence, of that day or hour no one knows, neither the angels in heaven, nor the Son, but the Father only.' He was ignorant in the special sense of making others ignorant—He did not know it among them in such a way as to reveal it to them at that time. In this way also it was said to Abraham: '*Now I know that you fear God*' (Genesis 22:12), meaning that Abraham himself came to know his own heart through testing. Jesus, likewise, withheld this knowledge from his disciples because they were not yet able to bear it."[1]

---

[1] St. Augustine of Hippo, "*On the Trinity*", Book 1, A.D. 399

In other words, Jesus' "ignorance" here does not imply a lack of divine knowledge, but a purposeful withholding of revelation.

This interpretation is reinforced by Acts 1:6–8, where the disciples asked the risen Christ:

"Lord, are you at this time going to restore the kingdom to Israel?" He said to them, 'It is not for you to know the times or dates the Father has set by his own authority." But you will receive power when the Holy Spirit comes upon you; and you will be my witnesses ... to the ends of the earth.'"

The timing of the end was not their concern. Instead, Jesus redirected them to the mission of receiving the Spirit and bearing witness to the gospel.

And indeed, they did. That is why we now know and proclaim the good news of Jesus Christ.

So, to conclude, Jesus has proven his omniscience on many recorded occasions. Therefore, this one occasion must be understood in the light of voluntarily concealing this knowledge as it didn't concern his disciples at that time.

Question 16

If the Bible is inspired by God's Holy Spirit, why would God allow contradictions to creep into His holy book?

For example, King Ahaziah's age is recorded as 22 in 2 Kings 8:26, but as 42 in 2 Chronicles 22:2.

Answer

Muslims often claim that the Bible is contradictory because it gives two different ages for Ahaziah when he became king.

It is important to note, however, that a true contradiction exists only when there is no possible way to reconcile two statements. If the seemingly conflicting statements address different aspects of an issue, use terms in different senses, or if there is any ambiguity surrounding facts presented, then it is unfair to charge a document with contradiction. A contradiction implies falsehood, and a historical narrative should be considered credible unless conclusively proven otherwise.

So let us examine the text to see if the two seemingly contradictory statements can be reconciled.

Scripture makes it clear that Ahaziah could not have been 42 years old when he became king, because his father, Jehoram, died at the age of 40 as we read:

"Jehoram was thirty-two years old when he became king, and he reigned in Jerusalem eight years. He passed away to no one's regret, and was buried in the City of David, but not in the tombs of the kings." (2 Chronicles 21:20)

The people of Judah made Ahaziah, Jehora's son, a king in his place (2 Chronicles 22:1). Therefore, it is impossible for Ahaziah to have been 42 years old at his coronation as he would have been older than his father! Clearly, according to the Scriptures, Ahaziah was 22, not 42, years old when he began to reign.

But why do the texts give two different figures?

Most scholars conclude that the figure in 2 Chronicles 22:2 is the result of a scribal error. There is a good reason for this view. Ancient Hebrews did not spell out numbers as we do today. Instead, they employed a system in which Hebrew letters represented numerical values. How far back this practice goes is debated, but evidence supports its antiquity.[1]

The problem is that several Hebrew letters look very similar, including those that represent twenty-two and forty-two. A very slight stroke of the pen could easily obscure the distinction.

If one objects that God could have miraculously prevented every scribal mistake, it must be remembered that such precise intervention would require continuous miraculous oversight throughout centuries of manuscript copying. Clearly, this was not God's plan for the preservation of Scripture. Haley presents an excellent discussion of scribal transmission.[2]

Additional support comes from ancient translations, many of which cast doubt on the "forty-two" reading. Most manuscripts of the Septuagint give twenty, and one has twenty-two. The Syriac and Arabic versions also record twenty-two. For this reason, several modern English translations (NASB, NIV, ESV) have corrected 2 Chronicles 22:2 to twenty-two.

Finally, it should be noted that the age of Ahaziah at the start of his reign has no impact whatsoever on any Jewish or Christian doctrine.

---

[1] Davis, John, "Biblical Numerology," Baker, 1968, p. 38
[2] Haley, John W. "Alleged Discrepancies of the Bible," 2004, pp. 19ff.

Whether he was 22 or 42 does not affect the authority, reliability, or message of Scripture.

So, to conclude, there is no real dispute on the age of King Ahaziah, as his age could be easily concluded from the Biblical text itself.

Question 17

If Jesus was truly, as Christians claim, a kind, respectful, and loving man, how could He call a human being a "dog" in Matthew 15?

Answer

Muslims often raise this question about Matthew 15:21–28:

"Leaving that place, Jesus withdrew to the region of Tyre and Sidon. A Canaanite woman from that vicinity came to him, crying out, 'Lord, Son of David, have mercy on me! My daughter is demon-possessed and suffering terribly.' Jesus did not answer a word. So his disciples came to him and urged him, 'Send her away, for she keeps crying out after us.' He answered, 'I was sent only to the lost sheep of Israel.' The woman came and knelt before him. 'Lord, help me!' she said. He replied, 'It is not right to take the children's bread and toss it to the dogs.'

'Yes, it is, Lord,' she said. 'Even the dogs eat the crumbs that fall from their master's table.'

Then Jesus said to her, 'Woman, you have great faith! Your request is granted.' And her daughter was healed at that moment."

(Matthew 15:21–28)

1. Jesus' Mission to Israel

In the Old Testament, God foretold that the *"man of sorrows"* (Isaiah 53:3) would suffer for His people—Israel.

John affirms, *"He came to His own, and His own did not receive Him."* (John 1:11)

Likewise, Jesus instructed His disciples:

"Do not go among the Gentiles." (Matthew 10:5)

Paul later explains:

"Jesus Christ has become a servant to the circumcision on behalf of the truth of God, to confirm the promises made to the fathers."

(Romans 15:8)

Thus, during His earthly ministry, Jesus' mission was first directed to Israel, in fulfillment of God's promises to Abraham and the prophets.

2. The Immediate Context

Just before this encounter, Jesus had taught that external things—such as food—cannot defile a person:

"What goes into someone's mouth does not defile them, but what comes out of their mouth, that is what defiles them."

(Matthew 15:11)

This teaching prepared His disciples to grasp that spiritual purity is not determined by ethnicity or ritual law. The encounter with the Canaanite (Syrophoenician) woman builds on this lesson.

3. Understanding Jesus' Words

At first glance, Jesus' reply—

"It is not right to take the children's bread and toss it to the dogs" (Matthew 15:26), may appear harsh, especially in English. However, the original Greek text clarifies His meaning.

In Jewish culture, Gentiles were often referred to as "dogs" using the word "kuōn," meaning "wild dog" or "stray" (Matthew 7:6; Philippians 3:2). This term carried strong connotations of uncleanness and contempt.

But Jesus does not use "kuōn" here. He instead uses the diminutive form "kunarion," meaning "little dog" or "household pet." The imagery is softened—it evokes not an insult, but a domestic metaphor. Just as a father feeds his children before the household pets, Jesus' earthly ministry was first directed to Israel before extending to the Gentiles.

4. A Test of Faith and a Lesson for the Disciples

Jesus' initial silence and His response were intentional. They tested the woman's faith and exposed the disciples' prejudice against Gentiles.

When Jesus said, *"I was sent only to the lost sheep of Israel"* (Matthew 15:24), He was articulating the current stage of His redemptive mission—not its ultimate scope. The woman's persistence, humility, and recognition of Jesus as *"Lord, Son of David"* revealed her deep faith. She accepted the metaphor and turned it into a confession:

"Even the dogs eat the crumbs that fall from their master's table." (Matthew 15:27)

Her faith mirrors the persistent widow in Luke 18:1–8, an example of unwavering trust in God despite apparent rejection.

Through this exchange, Jesus demonstrated to His disciples that faith—not race, status, or ritual purity—grants access to God's mercy. He commended her, saying,

"Woman, you have great faith!" (Matthew 15:28)

and healed her daughter instantly.

5. The True Meaning of the Passage

Far from insulting the woman, Jesus was leading both her and His disciples toward a revelation:

- That His compassion extends beyond Israel,
- That faith transcends ethnic boundaries, and
- That humility and perseverance are honoured by God.

What may seem like rejection was an invitation to deeper faith. The *"Canaanite woman"* becomes a powerful model of trust and persistence, and Jesus' response affirms her dignity and belief.

So, to conclude, this passage does not contradict Jesus' love, kindness, or respect for humanity. Instead, it displays His wisdom as a teacher.

He used the moment to:

- Test and reveal genuine faith,
- Challenge Jewish prejudice, and
- Foreshadow the inclusion of all nations in God's salvation plan.

Far from being an insult, Jesus' words opened the door to one of the clearest demonstrations of faith overcoming cultural barriers.

Through this encounter, Jesus revealed that God's mercy is for all who believe—Jew or Gentile, man or woman, slave or free.

Question 18

"Why do you criticize jihad, Islamic wars, when your own Bible is full of violent wars, where even children were slaughtered?", Muslims ask.

Answer

Firstly, not all the wars recorded in the Old Testament (and there are none in the New Testament) were divinely commanded. Some were simply political conflicts between tribes. What needs special consideration, however, is Israel's conquest of Canaan.

Below are 10 key differences between the warfare described in the Bible and Islamic jihad:

1. Purpose of Warfare

> Israel: The conquest of Canaan provided a homeland for a refugee nation. Israel had been enslaved in Egypt for 400 years (Genesis 15:13; Acts 7:6). God promised them land as a permanent home (Numbers 15:1)—not as territory to exploit for plunder.
>
> Islam: Jihad focused on expansion from Arabia, motivated by ideology and booty. The Qur'an says: *"He it is Who has sent His Messenger with guidance and the religion of truth, that He may make it prevail over all religion"* (Qur'an 9:33; 48:28; 61:9). Muhammad, the Prophet of Islam, said, "Allah made me wealthy through conquests."[1] Jihad aimed at spreading Islam's political, religious, and military rule.

2. Impetus for Warfare

> Israel: Many battles were defensive. Israel was attacked by the Amalekites (Exodus 17:8), the king of Heshbon (Numbers

21:23), five kings (Joshua 10:5), and others. Some wars were retaliatory (Numbers 25:16–18; 31:1–2).

Islam: Jihad was largely offensive. Muhammad sent ultimatums to peaceful nations such as Byzantium and Persia: *"If you accept Islam, you will be safe."*[2]

3. Goal of Warfare

Israel: The conquest was divine judgment on wicked nations. God delayed judgment until the *"sins of the Amorites had reached their full measure"* (Genesis 15:16). Canaanite practices such as child sacrifice (Deuteronomy 12:31) defiled the land (Leviticus 18:24–28).

Islam: The Qur'an commands Muslims to fight Jews and Christians until they submit and pay the jizya tax (Qur'an 9:29). Despite some verses of tolerance (Qur'an 2:62; 5:69), the dominant trajectory of Islamic law mandated the subjugation of non-Muslims.

4. Scope of Warfare

Israel: The conquest was geographically limited: *"I will establish your borders from the Red Sea to the Sea of the Philistines"* (Exodus 23:31).

Islam: jihad had a universal scope: *"Fight them until there is no more disbelief… and religion is entirely for Allah"* (Qur'an 8:39).

5. Targets of Warfare

Israel: Certain groups were off-limits (Deuteronomy 2:5, 9, 19, 37). Israelites were forbidden to fight their relatives or specific nations.

Islam: Prophet Muhammad said: *"I have been commanded to fight against the people until they testify that none has the right to be worshiped but Allah and that I am His Apostle."*[3]

6. Environmental Concerns

Israel: God forbade wanton destruction: *"Do not cut down fruit trees when you lay siege to a city"* (Deuteronomy 20:19).

Islam: Prophet Muhammad ordered the cutting of palm trees at Banu Nadir and vineyards at Ta'if.[4]

7. Divine Support

Israel: God fought against Israel when they disobeyed (Jeremiah 21:5; Exodus 22:22–24).

Islam: Allah is consistently said to fight for Muslims (Qur'an 3:13, 160; 33:25–26).

8. Consequences of Warfare

Israel: Wars had earthly consequences only (Nehemiah 4:14).

Islam: Martyrdom in jihad guaranteed Paradise (Qur'an 3:157; Sahih al-Bukhari 5:388). Prophet Muhammad said: *"If anyone meets Allah with no mark of jihad, he will meet Allah with a flaw in him."*[5]

9. Motivation

Israel: To secure religious freedom. Moses demanded of Pharaoh: *"Let my people go, so that they may worship me"* (Exodus 5:1). Israel's vision was a house of prayer for all nations (Isaiah 60:3).

Islam: To ensure Islam's supremacy. Prophet Muhammad said: "He who fights so that Allah's Word is supreme, fights in Allah's cause."[6]

10. Duration of Warfare

<u>Israel</u>: Old Testament warfare was temporary, limited to Israel's historical context (Deuteronomy 20:1–4). Prophets looked forward to peace: *"They shall beat their swords into ploughshares"* (Isaiah 2:4).

<u>Islam</u>: Jihad is ongoing. Prophet Muhammad said: *"Jihad will continue until the Day of Judgment."*[7]

So, to conclude, some Muslims cite wars from 3,000 years ago to justify present-day jihad. But the Old Testament wars were historically unique, geographically limited, and divinely judged. Islamic jihad, however, was commanded as a perpetual struggle until the whole world submits to Allah.

Therefore, the two are not parallel: Old Testament warfare has ended, while jihad continues.

---

[1] Sahih al-Bukhari, Hadith number 3:495

[2] Sahih al-Bukhari, Hadith numbers 1:6; 4:190–191

[3] Sahih al-Bukhari, Hadith number 1:24

[4] Qur'an 59:5, Ibn Ishaq, Sirat Rasul Allah, pp. 437, 589

[5] Sunan Tirmidhi, Book of Virtues, book 49, Chapter: The Virtues of 'Ali Ibn Abi Taleb, Hadith number 3835

[6] Sahih al-Bukhari, Hadith number 1:125

[7] Sunan Abu Dawud, Book of Prayer, book 2, Chapter on Recitation Out Loud, Hadith 1051; Qur'an 2:193

ANSWERS TO QUESTIONS

Question 19

Muslims often claim that Apostle Paul corrupted the pure teaching of Jesus.

This claim is based on a passage from the spurious and forged "Gospel of Barnabas":

"For certain evil men, pretending to be disciples, preached that Jesus died and rose again. Others preached, and yet preach, that Jesus is the son of God, among whom is Paul deceived." (Chapter 22)

Answer

A thorough investigation reveals that Jesus and Paul were in complete agreement on all major doctrines.

Below is a comparative summary demonstrating their harmony across key theological themes:

Further Revelation Through the Holy Spirit

In some matters, Paul expanded upon Jesus' foundation, as Jesus Himself foretold:

"I have much more to say to you, more than you can now bear. But when He, the Spirit of truth, comes, He will guide you into all the truth." (John 16:12–13)

For instance, regarding circumcision, Jesus addressed it briefly because His audience was predominantly Jewish and already circumcised:

"You circumcise on the Sabbath for the Law of Moses., Jesus said (John 7:22–23)

Paul, however, emphasized the spiritual meaning of circumcision, consistent with Old Testament teaching:

"Circumcise your hearts, therefore, and do not be stiff-necked any longer." (Deuteronomy 10:16)

"The Lord your God will circumcise your hearts… so that you may love Him." (Deuteronomy 30:6)

"Circumcise yourselves to the Lord." (Jeremiah 4:4)

"Circumcision is nothing and uncircumcision is nothing. Keeping God's commands is what counts." (1 Corinthians 7:19)

"Neither circumcision nor uncircumcision means anything; what counts is the new creation." (Galatians 6:15)

Slavery is another example. Jesus affirmed true freedom:

"If the Son sets you free, you will be free indeed." (John 8:36)

Paul condemned slave trading and affirmed equality in Christ:

"We are no longer slaves but brothers in the Lord." (Philemon 16; 1 Timothy 1:10)

So, to conclude, there are no contradictions between the teachings of Jesus and Paul. Paul's writings faithfully expand upon Jesus' message under the guidance of the Holy Spirit, confirming that the Apostle did not corrupt but clarified and continued Christ's teaching.

ANSWERS TO QUESTIONS

THEME	CONCEPT	TAUGHT BY JESUS	TAUGHT BY PAUL
Old Testament	Christianity is the fulfilment of Judaism	Matthew 5:18; Luke 16:16,17	Romans 10:4,9-11; Colossians 2:16,17
	Old Testament prophesied about Jesus	John 5:39; Luke 24:45-47	Romans 1:2; 1 Corinthians 15:3
Attitude to OT laws	Affirmed moral law	Matthew 5:18; Luke 18:18,19	Romans 7:16; 1 Timothy 1:8
	Ceremonial law cancelled	Mark 7:19	Romans 3:20; 6:14
	Opposition to legalism	Mark 2:23-28; 3:1-6	Galatians 2:16; 3:10-12
	Irrelevance of temple & rites	John 2:13-22; Mathew 12:6; 24:1,2	1 Corinthians 3:16,17; 2 Corinthians 6:16; Eph.2:21
Nature Of God	God is One	Mark 12:29	Romans 3:30
	Trinity: God is Father, Son & Holy Spirit	Matthew 28:19,20	Ephesians 1:17
	God the Father	John 5, 8, 10	Ephesians 3:14,15
	Jesus is the Son of God	John 10:36	Romans 1:4; Galatians 4:4
	Jesus & the Father	John 14:10	Colossians 1:19
	Jesus is the Messiah	Matthew 26:63	Acts 18:28

	Work of Holy Spirit	John 14-16	Romans 8:9; 12:3,4; 1Corinthians 6:9
Human Nature	People are created by God	Matthew 19:4	1Corinthians 15:48
	People are sinners	Mark 3:38; Matthew 12:34; John 2:24,25; 3:19,20	Romans 3:23
Person of Christ	Deity of Christ	John 10:30,36	Colossians 1:15,19; 2:9
	Pleased the Father not himself	John 5:40; 8:29	Romans 15:3
	Empowered by the Spirit	Luke 4:18,19	Romans 8:11
	Jesus had authority to forgive sin	Matthew 9:1-8; Mark 2:1-12; Luke 7:44-50	Ephesians 1:7; Colossians 1:14
	Jesus is the bridegroom of his church	Matthew 9:14-15; 22:1-13; 25:1-14	Ephesians 5:23-32
	Descended from but greater than David	Matthew 22:45; Mark 12:37; Luke 20:44	Romans 1:3
Christ's death & resurrection	Jesus died as an atonement for sin	Matthew 26:28; John 12:23	Ephesians 1:7; Romans 5:8; 1Corinthians 5:7
	Jesus died for others as a substitute	Mark 10:45; 14:24; Luke 22:19,20; John 10:11	2 Corinthians 5:21; Romans 4:25

ANSWERS TO QUESTIONS

	Jesus' death & burial completed by resurrection	Luke 24:46,47; John 20:25-29	Romans 10:9
	Defeated Satan	John 12:31; 16:11	Colossians 2:15
Response required	Man cannot save himself	Matthew 19:25,26; John 4:44	Ephesians 2:8,9
	Faith & surrender to Christ required	Mark 1:15; John 6:47	Romans 10:9,10
	Doing more than hearing	Luke 6:46	Romans 2:13
	Becoming a Jew not necessary	Matthew 8:5-13; 15:21-29; Luke 8:38,38; John 4: 21-24	Galatians 2:14,15
	Disciple all nations	Matthew 28:19,20	Romans 1:5; 16:26
Transformed life	Need to take up our cross	Luke 9:23	2 Corinthians 5:17
	A seed dies before it brings life	John 12:24	1 Corinthians 15:36
	The result is a changed life &commitment	Luke 14:25-35; John 15:1-11	2 Corinthians 5:17
	Be both wise and innocent	Matthew 10:16	Romans 16:19
	Primacy of love	John 15:9-17	I Corinthians 13; Rom.13:8-10.
Social &	Celibacy	Matthew 19:12	1 Corinthians 7:1,7

Ethical teaching	Monogamy	Matthew 19:4,5	Ephesians 5:31; 1 Timothy 3:2,12
	No divorce	Matthew 5:31; Mark 10:2-12	1Corinthians 7:11-13,27
	Don't judge others	Matthew 7:1-5	Romans 2:1-4
	Don't be men-pleasers	Matthew 6:1	Galatians 1:10
	Love your enemies	Luke 6:27; Matthew 5:43	Romans 12:14-21
Christ's return	Jesus will return	Matthew 24:30	1Thessalonians 1:10
	Jesus will judge everyone	Matthew 25:31-33	Acts 17:31
	Jesus will reward people	Matthew 16:27	Ephesians 6:8
	We will be forever with Him	John 14:3	1Thessalonians 4:17

Question 20

Quoting John 5:19, Muslims conclude that Jesus made it clear that He, by Himself, is powerless.

"Jesus gave them this answer: 'Very truly I tell you, the Son can do nothing by Himself; He can do only what He sees His Father doing, because whatever the Father does the Son also does.'" (John 5:19)

Answer

This verse is often misunderstood when taken out of its full context. In fact, John 5 presents the opposite of what Muslims claim. Far from declaring weakness or limitation, Jesus here reveals His divine unity and equality with God the Father in divine nature.

To grasp the meaning of John 5:19, we must read the preceding verses (John 5:16–18):

"So, because Jesus was doing these things on the Sabbath, the Jewish leaders began to persecute Him. In His defence Jesus said to them, 'My Father is always at His work to this very day, and I too am working.' For this reason, they tried all the more to kill Him; not only was He breaking the Sabbath, but He was even calling God His own Father, making Himself equal with God." (John 5:16–18)

The context makes it clear: Jesus was being accused of violating the Sabbath because He healed a man that day. His response— *"My Father is always at His work, and I too am working"*—asserts that just as God continues to sustain creation even on the Sabbath, Jesus likewise shares in the divine work of God. The Jews understood exactly what He meant, and for that reason, they sought to kill Him for claiming equality with God in divine nature.

"The Son can do nothing by Himself" — What it Really Means?

When Jesus said, "the Son can do nothing by Himself," He was not denying power or divinity. Rather, He was affirming perfect unity and harmony with the Father. He was emphasizing that He does nothing independently or separately from the Father's will.

In other words, Jesus was declaring: "I do not act apart from My Father; I act in complete oneness with Him."

This is not a statement of weakness, but a statement of divine cooperation.

Immediately after, Jesus continued:

"Whatever the Father does, the Son also does." (John 5:19)

Could any created being ever say that they can do whatever God does? Absolutely not. Such a statement would be blasphemous unless the speaker shared God's divine nature. Thus, Jesus was revealing His equality with the Father—not His inferiority.

Jesus the Divine Judge

Jesus' divine authority is further affirmed in the verses to follow:

"Moreover, the Father judges no one, but has entrusted all judgment to the Son, that all may honour the Son just as they honour the Father. Whoever does not honour the Son does not honour the Father, who sent Him." (John 5:22–23)

In the Old Testament, God alone is described as the ultimate Judge (Joel 3:12; Psalms 9:7–8).

The Qur'an, likewise, affirms that only God is the final Judge (Qur'an 5:48; 7:87; 10:109; 21:47).

Therefore, if the Father has entrusted all judgment to Jesus, we have two possibilities:

1. Either God gave His exclusive authority to a mere human being (which contradicts both the Bible and the Qur'an), or
2. Jesus truly shares the divine nature of God and is the rightful Judge of all humanity.

The second option is the only consistent interpretation.

Moreover, Jesus states that the Son deserves the same honour as the Father. Since one way to honour God is through worship, this passage reveals that Jesus is worthy of the same worship as God Himself.

Jesus' Divine Voice and Title

Jesus further declared:

"Very truly I tell you, a time is coming and has now come when the dead will hear the voice of the Son of Man, and those who hear will live." (John 5:25)

Only God can speak to the dead and give life. Yet Jesus claims that his own voice will raise the dead.

This statement directly connects to Daniel 7:13–14, where the Son of Man is a divine, heavenly figure who receives eternal dominion and worship.

When Jesus identified Himself as *"the Son of Man"* before the Jewish council (Mark 14:62; Matthew 26:64), they sentenced Him to death for blasphemy—because they understood that He was claiming divine status.

So, to conclude, far from teaching that Jesus was powerless, John 5 reveals His divine authority and unity with the Father.

- He performs the same work as God.
- He shares divine judgment.

- He receives equal honour and worship.
- He possesses life-giving power over the dead.

Thus, Jesus' words, rightly understood, affirm—not deny—His deity. He was not declaring weakness but revealing His oneness with the Almighty God.

Question 21

How could Jesus, the Prince of Peace, command His disciples to slaughter His enemies? (Luke 19:27)

Answer

Muslims often quote Luke 19:27 out of context to claim that Jesus commanded violence:

"But those enemies of mine who did not want me to be king over them—bring them here and kill them in front of me." (Luke 19:27)

However, a careful reading of the passage shows that this statement was part of a parable, not a command from Jesus. Context completely changes the meaning.

Understanding the Parable

Luke writes:

"While they were listening to this, he went on to tell them a parable, because he was near Jerusalem and the people thought that the kingdom of God was going to appear at once." (Luke 19:11)

Jesus told this parable to correct a misunderstanding. Many expected Him to immediately establish an earthly kingdom in Jerusalem. Instead, He used the parable to teach that the coming of His kingdom would involve a delay and accountability when He returns.

In the parable (Luke 19:12–27), a nobleman goes to a distant country to be appointed king and later returns to settle accounts with his servants. The citizens, however, reject his authority, saying, *"We don't want this man to be our king."* When he returns, he rewards the faithful servants and condemns the unfaithful. The story concludes with the line, *"Those enemies of mine who did not want me to be king over them—bring them here and kill them in front of me."*

This was not a literal command from Jesus to His followers. It was the conclusion of a story, illustrating what happens to those who reject the rightful king—symbolically referring to God's final judgment.

Historical Background

Jesus' listeners would have immediately recognized the political reference. The parable closely mirrors the story of Herod Archelaus, son of Herod the Great. After his father's death, Archelaus traveled to Rome to request confirmation from Emperor Augustus to rule over Judea. A Jewish delegation followed him to oppose his appointment, and upon his return, Archelaus punished his opponents severely.[1]

This recent historical event was still vivid in people's minds when Jesus uttered the parable and provided the backdrop for Jesus' parable. By using this familiar image, Jesus was not endorsing Archelaus' cruelty but teaching a spiritual truth: just as Archelaus returned to reign, so too would Jesus return as the rightful King to establish His kingdom and judge those who rejected Him.

Spiritual Meaning

The nobleman represents Christ, who would soon depart (through His death, resurrection, and ascension) and later return in glory. The servants represent believers, entrusted with spiritual resources ("minas") to invest in His kingdom. The unfaithful servant represents those who waste what God has given them, while the rebellious citizens symbolize those who reject Christ's authority.

---

[1] Flavius Josephus, *"Antiquities of the Jews."* Book 17, Retrieved 4 April 2020

Thus, the *"slaying of the enemies"* in Luke 19:27 symbolizes final divine judgment, not physical violence commanded by Jesus or His followers. Scripture consistently affirms that vengeance and judgment belong to God alone (Romans 12:19).

This interpretation is reinforced by Revelation 20:11–15, which describes the final judgment, when all who reject God will face eternal separation from Him:

"Then I saw a great white throne and him who was seated on it... Anyone whose name was not found written in the book of life was thrown into the lake of fire."

So, to conclude, Jesus, the Prince of Peace, never commanded His followers to use violence. The statement in Luke 19:27 is part of a parable illustrating the seriousness of rejecting Christ's kingship and the certainty of divine judgment at the end of time.

The message is not one of earthly warfare, but of spiritual accountability. Jesus calls His followers to peace, love, and faithfulness while warning that those who persistently reject Him will face just judgment from God.

Question 22

"The Trinity could never be explained to any logical mind. The word Trinity doesn't even exist in the Bible."

Some Muslims may even go further to say: "I will become a Christian if you can explain your Trinity to me."

Answer

As a quick response to the claim "The word Trinity isn't in the Bible," you can reply:

"The word *Tawheed* (The Oneness of God) isn't in the Qur'an either."

Muslims would rightly answer, "But it is clearly implied."

And you may respond: "Exactly—and so is the Trinity."

God Is Incomparable and Unique

Both the Bible and the Qur'an affirm that God is beyond comparison.

"I am God, and there is none like Me." (Isaiah 46:9; 45:5; 43:11)
"To whom will you compare Me or count Me equal? To whom will you liken Me that we may be compared?" (Isaiah 46:5; 40:18)
"There is nothing whatsoever like unto Him." (Qur'an 42:11)

Our Problem: Human Limitations

When we speak about God, we are bound by human language and human thought.

Can finite minds ever fully describe an infinite and majestic God? Of course not.

The Solution: God's Revelation

Both the Bible and the Qur'an affirm that God reveals truths to humanity that we could never discover on our own:

"It is not granted to any mortal that God should speak to him except through revelation, or from behind a veil, or by sending a messenger to command what He wills: He is exalted and wise." (Qur'an 42:51)

"The secret things belong to the LORD our God, but the things revealed belong to us and to our children forever." (Deuteronomy 29:29)

God's Self-Description

In the Qur'an, God refers to Himself using both singular and plural forms, and across different grammatical persons:

First person singular: "I" or "Me" (Qur'an 2:30, 33, 38, 40)

First person plural: "We" or "Our" (Qur'an 2:34–39)

Third person: "He" or "Him" (Qur'an 2:31, 33)

Second person: "You" or "Your" (Qur'an 2:30, 32)

God also reveals Himself through many names. God has ninety-nine names.[1]

The Bible, in turn, gives over 240 names and titles for God — demonstrating His depth and complexity.

Clearly, God is not simple; He is infinitely rich in being and attributes.

God Is One

---

[1] Sahih al-Bukhari, Hadith number 3:894

Both the (Qur'an 112:1) and the Bible (Deuteronomy 6:4; Mark 12:29) proclaim that "God is one."

However, the Bible uses two Hebrew words for "one":

Yachid – meaning a solitary, single one.

Echad – meaning a composite unity, a oneness made of multiple parts.

For example:

"The two shall become one (echad) flesh." (Genesis 2:24) *Ezekiel joined two sticks so that they became "one (echad) in his hand."* (Ezekiel 37:17)

The Shema (Deuteronomy 6:4) uses *echad*, not *yachid* — implying that God's oneness is complex, not solitary.

Examples of Complex Unity

We see many analogies of unity within diversity in creation itself:

Biology: An amoeba is a simple unity, but the human body is a complex unity — many cells, one organism.

Geometry: A straight line is simple; a cube or sphere is a complex unity — one object, three dimensions.

Society: Families, teams, and nations are unities composed of many members.

Thus, unity does not necessarily mean absolute singularity.

The Concept of Three-in-One

Trinity means three Divine Persons sharing one Divine Essence.

We see similar patterns of *"three-in-one"* in the natural world:

Time: Past, present, future — yet one continuum.

Space: Length, width, height — yet one space.

Matter: Solid, liquid, gas — yet one substance.

Atoms: Protons, neutrons, electrons — yet one atom.

Some object using arithmetic: "1 + 1 + 1 = 3." But another equation is equally valid: $1 \times 1 \times 1 = 1$. God is not a mathematical formula — He transcends all human categories.

The Trinity in Scripture

Jesus commanded His followers:

"Baptize them in the name [singular] of the Father, and of the Son, and of the Holy Spirit." (Matthew 28:19)

When Jesus said,

"The Father and I are one" (John 10:30)

He used the Greek word "hen" (neuter, meaning "one essence"), not "heis" (masculine, "one person").

Thus, Jesus claimed unity of essence, not identity of person.

The Father, Son, and Holy Spirit are distinct Persons — yet one God.

The Divine Attributes Shared by All Three

Attribute	Father (e.g.)	Son (e.g.)	Spirit (e.g.)
Eternal	Romans 16:26-27	Romans 1:17	Hebrews 9:14
Creator	Psalms 100:3	Colossians 1:16	Psalms 104:30
Omnipresent	Jeremiah 23:24	Ephesians 1:23	Psalms 139:7

Attribute	Father (e.g.)	Son (e.g.)	Spirit (e.g.)
Omniscient	1 John 3:20	John 21:17	1 Corinthians 2:10
Gives Life	Genesis 1:11–31	John 1:4; 5:21	Romans 8:10–11
Strengthens	Psalms 138:3	Philippians 4:13	Ephesians 3:16
Is Light	James 1:17	John 8:12	2 Corinthians 4:6
Is Love	John 16:27	John 14:21	Romans 5:5

Each Person is fully God, sharing the same divine attributes.

Why Trinity Matters

1. God Is Love

Love requires a relationship. Before creation, love already existed within the Godhead — between the Father, Son, and Spirit (John 17:24).

2. God Saves Through Divine Cooperation
- The Father sends the Son (John 3:16).
- The Son enters the world as the Word made flesh (John 1:14).
- The Spirit empowers and sustains the Son (Luke 4:18; Qur'an 2:87, 2:253). Salvation is a work of the Triune God acting in perfect unity.

3. God Meets Us in Every Way
- The Father is God for us — the One who sends.
- The Son is God with us — Emmanuel, who dies for us.
- The Spirit is God in us — who transforms and gives new life (2 Corinthians 3:18).

So, to conclude, Trinity reveals that God is relational, loving, and active.

Far from being "illogical" or "nonsense," Trinity expresses the deepest truth about God's nature and His relationship with humanity.

While the word Trinity, as such, is not found in the Bible, the concept permeates Scriptures from beginning to end — just as Tawheed (Oneness of God) is implied throughout the Qur'an.

Question 23

"The Trinity is an invention of Apostle Paul in the New Testament, since it has no mention in the Old Testament." Isn't that so? Muslims ask.

Answer

The doctrine of the Trinity is not an invention of Apostle Paul. In fact, the Old Testament contains numerous references that describe, suggest, or point toward the Triune nature of God — one God revealed as Father, Son, and Holy Spirit.

1) The Name Used for "God"

A common name for God in the Old Testament is Elohim, used 2,606 times (second only to Yahweh, used 6,519 times). Elohim is a plural noun (its singular form is Eloah), yet it consistently appears with singular verbs, implying unity.

"In the beginning God (Elohim – plural) created (bara – singular) the heavens and the earth." (Genesis 1:1)

This grammatical combination — a plural noun with a singular verb — reflects plurality in unity, serving as a linguistic hint toward the triune nature of God.

2) God Sometimes Speaks in the Plural

"Let us make man in our image." (Genesis 1:26)

"Come, let us go down and confuse their language." (Genesis 11:7)

These divine self-references in the plural form suggest a conversation within the Godhead.

3) The Shema: Unity in Diversity

The Shema (Deuteronomy 6:4) is the central confession of Jewish faith, comparable to the Shahada in Islam:

"Hear, O Israel: The LORD our God, the LORD is one."

Jesus quoted this verse when asked about the greatest commandment (Mark 12:29).

The Hebrew word translated "one" is "echad," meaning a composite unity — the same word used in Genesis 2:24 when husband and wife become "one" flesh.

Had Moses intended to express absolute singularity, he would have used "yachid", which denotes a numerical oneness and is never used for God[1].

Thus, "echad" allows for unity within plurality, consistent with the Trinitarian understanding of God.

4) God as Father

God is described as Father or depicted in paternal terms roughly 25 times in the Old Testament (e.g., Deuteronomy 32:6; Isaiah 63:16; 64:8; Jeremiah 3:4, 19; 31:9; Malachi 1:6; 2:10).

He is also called the Father of specific individuals (2 Samuel 7:14; 1 Chronicles 17:13; 22:10; 28:6; Psalms 68:5; 89:26).

Even when the term itself is absent, the imagery remains — as in Exodus 4:22–23; Deuteronomy 1:31; Psalms 103:13; Hosea 11:1–4.

5) The "Son" of God in the Old Testament

The Old Testament also refers to the Son, closely associated with God:

- 2 Samuel 7:14 – *"He will be a son to me."*

- Psalms 2:7–9 *"You are my Son… Kiss the Son."*
- Proverbs 30:4 – *"Who has ascended to heaven… what is His Son's name?"*
- Daniel 7:13–14 – *"One like the Son of Man, coming with the clouds of heaven."*

These texts prophetically anticipate the divine Son revealed in the New Testament.

6) Christophanies: Pre-Incarnate Appearances of Christ

In the Old Testament, God sometimes appeared in visible form as "the Angel (Messenger) of the LORD." These manifestations, known as Christophanies, are understood as appearances of the pre-incarnate Christ. Early Church Father Justin Martyr (d. 165) wrote: *"No one ever saw the Father, but the One who appeared to Abraham, to Jacob, and to Moses was He who is called God and Lord, the Son of God."*[2]

Examples include:

- "The LORD God walking in the garden" (Genesis 3:8)
- The Angel of the LORD appearing to Hagar (Genesis 16:7–13)
- The LORD appearing to Abraham (Genesis 17:1; 18:1; 22:11–12)
- Jacob wrestling with God (Hosea 12:2–5)
- The burning bush (Exodus 3:4–6; Qur'an 20:10–17)
- The Commander of the LORD's army (Joshua 5:13–6:2)
- The Angel of the LORD appearing to Samson's parents (Judges 13:6–22)

7) The God Who Can Be Seen and the God Who Cannot

Scripture distinguishes between the invisible God (the Father) and God's visible manifestation (the Son):

"You cannot see my face, for no one may see me and live." (Exodus 33:20)

"The LORD would speak to Moses face to face, as a man speaks with his friend." (Exodus 33:11)

The New Testament clarifies:

"No one has ever seen God, but God the One and Only, who is at the Father's side, has made him known." (John 1:18)
"He is the image of the invisible God." (Colossians 1:15)

8) Prophecies of the Divine Messiah

The Old Testament contains nearly 400 prophecies fulfilled in Jesus Christ. Among them, one explicitly describes the coming Messiah as "Mighty God."

"For to us a child is born, to us a Son is given... and his name shall be called Wonderful Counsellor, Mighty God, Everlasting Father, Prince of Peace." (Isaiah 9:6)

9) The Spirit of God

The Spirit of God or Holy Spirit is mentioned about 94 times in the Old Testament.

These references align perfectly with New Testament teaching about the Holy Spirit as a divine Person, not merely a force.

10) The Three Persons Together

Several Old Testament passages mention all three divine Persons together:

(a) Isaiah 48:12–16 – The Messiah speaks of being sent by "the Sovereign LORD" and "His Spirit."

(b) Isaiah 61:1–2 – *"The Spirit of the Sovereign LORD is upon me, because the LORD has anointed me…"*

(c) Isaiah 63:8–10 – God the Father, the Savior (the Son), and the Holy Spirit are all distinctly mentioned.

In Genesis 1:1–4, we see God who creates, His Word who speaks creation into being, and His Spirit hovering over the waters.

So, to conclude, the doctrine of the Trinity is not a New Testament innovation, but a progressive revelation of the eternal nature of God — Father, Son, and Holy Spirit — consistently revealed throughout Scripture.

From Genesis to Revelation, the Bible presents one God in a complex unity: three divine Persons sharing one essence.

---

[1] Brown, M. *Answering Jewish Objections to Jesus*, Vol. 2 (2000)

[2] Martyr, Justin, *"Dialogue with Trypho"*, Chapter 56, AD 155-160

Question 24

How could Jesus, the Prince of Peace, according to Christian beliefs, ask His disciples to purchase swords for fighting and killing?

"He said to them, 'But now if you have a purse, take it, and also a bag; and if you don't have a sword, sell your cloak and buy one.'"

(Luke 22:36)

Answer

Jesus is indeed the Prince of Peace, who came not to spread violence but to bring love, healing, and salvation. So, what, then, did He mean when He instructed His disciples to buy swords in Luke 22:36?

When the disciples heard His request, they responded: *"See, Lord, here are two swords."* (Luke 22:38). Later that same night, in Gethsemane, Peter used one of those swords to cut off the ear of Malchus, the servant of the high priest (Luke 22:50; John 18:10).

However, instead of commending Peter, Jesus rebuked him:

"Put your sword back in its place, for all who draw the sword will die by the sword." (Matthew 26:52)

He, then, healed the injured man (Luke 22:51). Clearly, Jesus was not calling His followers to commit violence.

When the disciples presented the two swords, Jesus replied, *"Enough of this!"* (Luke 22:38). Was He implying that two small weapons could protect Him from a fully armed Roman cohort? Absolutely not. Jesus Himself declared:

"Do you think I cannot call on My Father, and He will at once put at My disposal more than twelve legions of angels?"
(Matthew 26:53)

He had infinite heavenly power at His command.

So why, then, did Jesus ask his disciples to buy swords?

To understand Luke 22:36, we must read the verse that followed (v. 37)

"It is written: 'And he was numbered with the transgressors'; and I tell you that this must be fulfilled in me. Yes, what is written about me is reaching its fulfillment." (Luke 22:37, quoting Isaiah 53:12)

Jesus was preparing His disciples for a time of trial and persecution. His words were symbolic, representing the need to be ready for hostility and danger. The swords were not intended for fighting but to fulfill prophecy and remind the disciples of the opposition they would soon face.

Earlier, when Jesus sent the disciples out to preach, He told them:

"Take nothing for the journey—no staff, no bag, no bread, no money, no extra shirt." (Luke 9:3; 10:4)

At that stage, they enjoyed public favor and hospitality. But now, as His arrest and crucifixion approached, circumstances had changed. Darkness was about to descend. Hostility, not welcome, awaited them.

Thus, His instruction to "buy a sword" was a figurative warning: *Be prepared—times of danger are coming.*

The two swords they possessed could offer only minimal defense or deterrence against aggressors. Jesus willingly gave His life, but His disciples needed to protect themselves enough to continue their mission of spreading the gospel to all nations.

Nevertheless, the broader teaching of Jesus was unmistakable: the sword was not His way. Peter, who once drew a weapon in misguided zeal, later laid down his life for Christ, crucified upside down—just as his Master foretold. (John 21:18)

The two swords mentioned in Luke 22:36 were certainly not intended for offensive warfare against the Romans—the most powerful army of the time—but served as a symbolic and minimal means of self-defense amid rising hostility.

So, to conclude, Jesus never initiated, commanded, or commended violence. Even the Qur'an affirms His peaceful nature, quoting Him as saying in His infancy:

"Peace be upon me the day I was born, the day I die, and the day I will be raised back to life." (Qur'an 19:33)

Question 25

How could you believe that Jesus is God when He says that He has a God in John 20:17?

"*Jesus said to her, 'Do not cling to me, for I have not yet ascended to the Father; but go to my brothers and say to them, "I am ascending to my Father and your Father, to my God and your God."*

(John 20:17)

Answer

The above verse are the words of the risen Jesus, spoken to Mary Magdalene after His resurrection.

The first thing to notice is that Jesus did not say, "I am ascending to our Father and our God." Instead, He deliberately distinguished "My Father and your Father" and "My God and your God."

Also, when Muslims cite this verse, they are admitting that these are indeed the words of the resurrected Jesus, thereby affirming His resurrection — a truth the Qur'an itself denies.

Let us now examine the passage carefully and consider its meaning.

1. Jesus' Deity Affirmed by Thomas

A few verses later, in the same chapter, we read about Thomas, one of Jesus' disciples, who had doubted the resurrection until he personally saw the risen Christ:

"*Then he said to Thomas, 'Put your finger here; see my hands. Reach out your hand and put it into my side. Stop doubting and believe." Thomas said to him, 'My Lord and my God!' Then Jesus told him, 'Because you have seen me, you have believed; blessed are those who have not seen and yet have believed.'"* (John 20:27–29)

Here, Thomas directly calls Jesus "My Lord and my God."

If Jesus were not divine, He would have corrected Thomas immediately — but He did not. Instead, Jesus accepted this declaration of faith and pronounced a blessing upon all who would likewise believe.

The Greek words used for *"Lord" (Kyrios)* and *"God" (Theos)* in verse 28 are the same as those found in John 20:17 — the verse under discussion.

This demonstrates that the terms applied to the God of Israel are also rightly applied to Jesus Christ.

2. The One Lord and One God of Israel

Scripture consistently declares that Israel has only one Lord and one God:

"Hear, O Israel: The Lord our God, the Lord is one. Love the Lord your God with all your heart and with all your soul and with all your strength." (Deuteronomy 6:4–5)

The titles *"Lord"* and *"God"* — reserved for Yahweh — are now ascribed to Jesus. Therefore, calling Jesus both Lord and God affirms His divine identity, not a contradiction of it.

As discussed in Question 1 in this book, several divine titles that belong exclusively to Yahweh, the God of the Bible, and to Allah, the God of the Qur'an, are also applied to Jesus in the New Testament.

3. The Unique Relationship Between the Father and the Son

Returning to John 20:17, Jesus distinguishes His relationship to God from that of His disciples.

"I am ascending to My Father and your Father, to My God and your God."

Jesus is revealing that His sonship is unique. God is His Father in a way that He is not the Father of others.

The Gospel of John opens by affirming Jesus' eternal nature:

"In the beginning was the Word, and the Word was with God, and the Word was God."   (John 1:1)

And later:

"The Word became flesh and made His dwelling among us. We have seen His glory, the glory of the one and only Son, who came from the Father, full of grace and truth."   (John 1:14)

It was not the Father who became flesh, nor the Holy Spirit — it was the Son, the eternal Word, who took on human nature and lived in obedience to the Father's will (Mark 10:45).

4. The Meaning of "One and Only Son"

"For God so loved the world that He gave His one and only Son, that whoever believes in Him shall not perish but have eternal life."

(John 3:16)

The Greek term translated *"one and only"* is monogenēs, which means unique, one of a kind, or of the same nature.

This expresses Jesus' exclusive sonship — He shares the very nature of the Father.

That is why Jesus said, *"My Father and your Father."*

Believers become children of God by adoption (John 1:12), but Jesus is the Son by nature and essence.

5. Jesus' Humanity and Deity

When Jesus referred to the Father as "My God," He spoke as the incarnate Son — fully human and fully obedient to His Father's will.

As the eternal Word, He had always been with God and was God, but in His humanity, He acknowledged the Father as His God, demonstrating perfect obedience and submission within the divine plan of salvation.

So, to conclude, Jesus' words in John 20:17 do not deny His deity — they affirm His twofold nature.

As God, He shares the Father's essence.

As man, He perfectly submits to the Father's will.

Thus, Jesus is both fully God and fully man, the eternal Word made flesh — the divine Son who calls the Father "My God" in His humanity and "My Father" in His eternal divinity.

Question 26

How could Jesus be God when He prayed to God?

Answer

Muslims often raise this question on the assumption that prayer always equals worship.

However, that assumption is incorrect — even the Qur'an itself shows that "prayer" can have other meanings.

"Indeed, Allah and His angels pray upon the Prophet. O you who have believed, ask [Allah to confer] blessing upon him and ask [Allah to grant him] peace." (Qur'an 33:56)

The Arabic word translated *"pray"* here is يصلّون (yusallūna) — literally, *"they pray."*

Does this mean that Allah worships Prophet Muhammad when He prays upon him? Of course not.

In this context, praying upon means to bless, honour, or show favor, not to worship.

Therefore, prayer in its broader sense can mean blessing, glorifying, interceding, or expressing fellowship — not necessarily worship.

1. Prayer Is Relational, Not Just Worship

When Christians pray to God, they are not only worshiping in the sense of a creature adoring its Creator; but they are also engaging in communion with Him — glorifying, thanking, and aligning themselves with His will.

So if Jesus, the Son, prays to the Father, it is perfectly consistent with His divine nature as a distinct Person within the Trinity.

The Father is not the Son, the Son is not the Spirit, and the Spirit is not the Father — yet all three are one God in perfect unity.

From eternity, the Father, the Son, and the Holy Spirit have existed in an unbroken relationship of love, honour, and glorification toward one another.

2. Mutual Glorification Within the Trinity

- The Father glorifies the Son:

"And a voice came from heaven: 'You are my Son, whom I love; with you I am well pleased.'" (Mark 1:11)

- The Son glorifies the Father:

"Your throne, O God, will last for ever and ever; a scepter of justice will be the scepter of your kingdom. You have loved righteousness and hated wickedness; therefore, God, your God, has set you above your companions by anointing you with the oil of joy."

(Hebrews 1:8–9, quoting Psalm 45)

Here, the Father calls the Son "God", while the Son glorifies His Father — showing divine reciprocity, not subordination.

"Father, the hour has come. Glorify your Son, that your Son may glorify you." (John 17:1)

And elsewhere Jesus says:

"I am not seeking glory for myself, but there is one who seeks it, and he is the judge." (John 8:50)

Here, the Father actively seeks to glorify the Son.

- The Spirit intercedes in prayer:

"The Spirit himself intercedes for us through wordless groans. And he who searches our hearts knows the mind of the Spirit, because

the Spirit intercedes for God's people in accordance with the will of God." (Romans 8:26–27)

- The Spirit glorifies the Son:

"He will glorify me because it is from me that he will receive what he will make known to you. All that belongs to the Father is mine. That is why I said the Spirit will receive from me what he will make known to you." (John 16:14–15)

3. The Logic of the Trinity

If one argues that Jesus cannot be God because He prayed to the Father, then — by the same reasoning — the Father who glorifies the Son, and the Spirit who intercedes, could also not be God. But Scripture clearly reveals that all three Persons of the Godhead honour, glorify, and commune with one another in perfect unity.

Thus, prayer within the Trinity is not an act of worship from a lesser to a greater being, but rather an expression of eternal love and communion within the divine relationship.

So, to conclude, Jesus' prayers to the Father do not contradict His divinity. Rather, they reveal the intimate fellowship that has always existed between the Father, the Son, and the Holy Spirit.

Within the eternal Trinity, communication, intercession, and glorification are acts of divine unity, not signs of inferiority.

Therefore, Jesus praying to the Father is not evidence against His deity — it is a beautiful demonstration of it.

Question 27

"Jesus was surely a Muslim—He prayed like a Muslim and fasted like a Muslim." (Matthew 26:36–42 and Luke 22:39–42.) Why, then, wouldn't Christians follow the example of Jesus and become Muslims?

Answer

Muslims frequently point to the scene in Gethsemane (Matthew 26:36–42; Luke 22:39–42) as evidence that Jesus prayed "like a Muslim." A typical citation reads:

"Then Jesus went with his disciples to a place called Gethsemane... Going a little farther, he fell on his face and prayed, 'My Father, if it is possible, may this cup be taken from me. Yet not as I will, but as you will.'... 'Watch and pray so that you will not fall into temptation. The spirit is willing, but the flesh is weak.'" (Matthew 26:36–42)

Muslims usually emphasize verse 39 — *"He fell on his face and prayed"* — and conclude, "See, Jesus prostrated like a Muslim."

However, a closer reading of the context, as well as a comparison of theological meaning and practices, show that this conclusion does not hold.

1. Context and Address: "My Father…"

In Gethsemane, Jesus addresses God as "My Father." This is theologically profound — it reflects a unique filial relationship between Jesus and God, one that the Qur'an explicitly denies (Qur'an 6:101; 9:30; 19:88–93).

Thus, the key point is not Jesus' posture of prayer but His relationship with God. Jesus prays as the Son to His Father — a central theme throughout the Gospels (John 10:30; John 20:17).

This relational intimacy has no parallel in Islamic theology, which rejects any notion of divine sonship.

2. Posture and Style in Scripture

The Bible shows that Jesus prayed in a variety of ways — sometimes standing, sometimes kneeling, sometimes prostrating, and sometimes looking up to heaven.

Examples include:

- Private prayer: *"But when you pray, go into your room, close the door and pray to your Father, who is unseen."* (Matthew 6:6)
- Avoiding vain repetition: *"And when you pray, do not keep on babbling like pagans."* (Matthew 6:7)
- Public intercession: Jesus' High Priestly prayer (John 17)
- Thanksgiving: *"Then Jesus looked up and said, 'Father, I thank you that you have heard me.'"* (John 11:41–42)

Thus, while Jesus at times fell on His face in humility, this was not part of a fixed, formalized ritual like the Muslim salah (prayer). The posture expresses submission, but the theology and context behind the act are distinct.

3. Fasting: Jesus' Forty-Day Fast vs. Ramadan

Muslims fast during the month of Ramadan from dawn to sunset for a lunar month. Jesus' fast, however, was very different:

"He ate nothing during those days, and at the end of them he was hungry." (Luke 4:1–2)

Jesus' fast lasted forty continuous days, not daily intervals. Its purpose was spiritual preparation for His public ministry and confrontation with temptation — not ritual observance.

Moreover, Jesus taught that fasting should be discreet and inward, not a public display:

"When you fast, do not look somber as the hypocrites do... But when you fast, put oil on your head and wash your face." (Matthew 6:16–18)

Therefore, both the nature and purpose of Jesus' fasting differ radically from the Islamic practice of the month of Ramadan.

4. Purpose and Theology Matter More than External Similarity

Even when certain actions appear outwardly similar — such as bowing, prostrating, or abstaining from food — the meaning and motivation are completely different.

Jesus' prayer and fasting arose from:

- His Jewish background,
- His Messianic mission, and
- His divine sonship and obedience to the Father's redemptive will.

These actions were not rooted in the teachings of Muhammad, who lived over six centuries later.

To claim that Jesus was a Muslim simply because He prayed and fasted confuses external resemblance with theological identity.

So, to conclude, although Jesus prayed and fasted, His prayer and fasting were grounded in His identity as the incarnate Son of God and the Jewish Messiah, not as a follower of Islam.

His relationship with the Father, His manner of prayer, and His purpose in fasting all reflect a theology utterly distinct from Islamic belief.

A careful and honest reading of the Gospels shows that the outward actions of Jesus and Muslims may occasionally look alike, but their intent, purpose, and theology are entirely different.

Therefore, the claim that "Jesus was a Muslim" is based on a superficial comparison, not on the deeper reality of who Jesus truly is.

Question 28

Why don't Christians believe that Jesus was not crucified, when the Gospel of Barnabas confirms it?

Wasn't Barnabas a ministry partner of Apostle Paul and contemporary of Jesus? Didn't he write the Gospel that bears his name?

Answer

This question requires an examination of the so-called Gospel of Barnabas and its historical reliability. Was it truly written by Barnabas, the companion of Apostle Paul, who lived in the first century?

Barnabas, originally named Joseph (Acts 4:36), was a Levite from Cyprus and a close associate of Apostle Paul. He accompanied Paul on his first missionary journey (Acts 11:30–12:25; 14:43–50). If Barnabas had written a gospel, it would have been composed in the first century, during the same period as the canonical Gospels.

However, the earliest known manuscripts of the Gospel of Barnabas date only from the 14th to 17th century A.D.—about 1,400 years after Jesus. Unlike the canonical Gospels, which are preserved in over 5,300 Greek manuscripts, alone, this work exists in only two manuscripts, an Italian and a Spanish, that are dated back to 14th - 17th century.[1]

Muslims and Historical Awareness

Although the Gospel of Barnabas agrees with the Qur'an's claim that Jesus was not crucified, it was unknown to early Muslim scholars. Between the 7th and 15th centuries, prominent writers such as Ibn Hazm al-Andalusi (d. 1094), Ibn Taymiyyah (d. 1328), and Ibn Jarir al-Tabari (d. 923) made no mention of this work.[2]

In fact, the Gospel of Barnabas contains teachings that contradict both the Qur'an and the Bible. For example, it denies that Jesus is the Messiah and instead applies this title to Prophet Muhammad—something the Qur'an itself does not teach.

Because of such inconsistencies, many Muslim scholars rejected the book's authenticity. Among them are:

- Dr. Abbas Al-Aqqad, Egyptian journalist and literary critic (d. 1964)[3].
- Dr. Mohammad Ghorbal, Egyptian historian (d. 1961).[4]
- Mohammad Gibril, an Egyptian journalist, wrote "Most Muslim scholars deny the authenticity of this gospel, despite its apparent agreement with the Qur'an about the crucifixion."[5]

Evidence of Late Origin

The Gospel of Barnabas contains numerous historical, geographical, and theological errors that clearly show it could not have been written by a first-century eyewitness.[6]

1. Geographical Errors

- Chapter 22 states: *"Jesus went up to Capernaum from Nazareth."*
  In reality, Capernaum lies below Nazareth, near the Sea of Galilee. This demonstrates ignorance of the region.
- Chapter 20 states: *"Jesus went down to the Sea of Galilee and sailed to his town, Nazareth."*

Nazareth is inland, built on a hill—not a coastal town.

By contrast, Luke accurately records that Nazareth was "built on a hill" (Luke 4:28–30).

2. Historical Errors

Chapters 152 and 154 describe Roman soldiers debating Jesus inside the Jewish temple—an almost impossibility, since pagans were forbidden to enter the temple (Acts 10:28).

3. Theological Contradictions

- In John 1:19–23, John the Baptist denies being the Messiah, Elijah, or the Prophet.

But Chapter 42 of the Gospel of Barnabas claims that Jesus denies being the Messiah and applies Isaiah's prophecy to John the Baptist—reversing their biblical roles.

- The same chapter, Chapter 42, records Jesus as saying that he is "unworthy to untie the sandals" of the Prophet who comes after him—words that John the Baptist actually spoke about Jesus (John 1:27).

This confusion exposes the author's misunderstanding of Scripture.

4. Doctrinal Errors

- Chapter 35 teaches that the spirit of Muhammad was created 60,000 years before anything else—a teaching found in neither the Qur'an nor authentic hadith.
- Chapter 36 bizarrely claims that man's navel was created from Satan's spit, an idea unknown to any sacred text.

So, to conclude, the so-called Gospel of Barnabas is not trustworthy.

It was not written by Barnabas, the companion of Paul, but by an anonymous medieval author—likely in the period 14th to 17th century. It contains serious historical, geographical, and theological errors, and it contradicts both the Bible and the Qur'an.

Many Muslim scholars have dismissed it as unauthentic.

Therefore, Christians reject the Gospel of Barnabas not because it contradicts their faith, but because it fails every test of historical reliability.

---

[1] Joosten, J. *"The Date and Provenance of the "Gospel of Barnabas""*. The Journal of Theological Studies. **61** (1), p. 200–215, 2010.

[2] Geisler, Norman; Saleeb, Abdul *(1993)*. *"Answering Islam: The Crescent in Light of the Cross."* Baker Books, 1993.

[3] Al-Akhbar Newspaper (An Egyptian Newspaper), 26th October, 1959.

[4] *"The Simplified Arabic Encyclopedia,"* under the title "Barnabas", Cairo, Egypt, 2009.

[5] *"The Egyptian Evening Journal,"* 19th May, 2023.

[6] Joosten, J. *"The Date and Provenance of the "Gospel of Barnabas""*. The Journal of Theological Studies. **61** (1), p. 200–215, 2010.

Question 29

Jesus said: "My Father is greater than I." (John 14:28) So how could Jesus be God or possess a divine nature if He clearly stated that the Father is greater than Him?

Answer

This argument misunderstands the meaning of the word "greater." In both Greek and English, greater can refer to two different things:

1. Greatness in essence or nature, and
2. Greatness in position, role, or rank.

For example:

- If someone says, *"I am greater than my dog,"* the difference lies both in essence (human vs. animal) and rank.
- If someone says, *"My boss is greater than I,"* the difference is one of position or authority, not of essence, since both share the same human nature.

So, when Jesus said, *"My Father is greater than I,"* was He speaking about nature or about role? The context shows He was referring to role and position, not to divine nature.

Earlier in the same chapter, Jesus declared:

"Very truly I tell you, whoever believes in me will do the works I have been doing, and they will do even greater things than these, because I am going to the Father. And I will do whatever you ask in my name, so that the Father may be glorified in the Son." (John 14:12–14)

The same Greek word for "greater" (*meizōn*) appears in both verse 12 and verse 28. In verse 12, "greater works" clearly does not mean "better in quality" but *greater in scope or quantity*. Likewise, in verse 28, *"the Father is greater"* refers to rank—not essence.

On many occassions, Jesus made it clear that he was sent by the Father to do the works that the Father assigned to him to do:-

"I have testimony weightier than that of John. For the works that the Father has given me to finish—the very works that I am doing—testify that the Father has sent me." (John 5:36)

" For I have come down from heaven not to do my will but to do the will of him who sent me." (John 6:38)

On another occassion, Jesus said that the messenger can not be greater than the one who sent him. (John 13:16)

So, it is obvious that the greatness here is in status and not in nature.

Within this very passage Jesus also makes claims that reveal His divine status:

1. Jesus answers prayer

"I will do whatever you ask in my name ... You may ask me for anything in my name, and I will do it." (John 14:13–14)

To hear and respond to all prayers requires omniscience, omnipresence, and omnipotence—attributes belonging only to God.

2. Jesus shares God's indwelling presence

"Anyone who loves me will obey my teaching. My Father will love them, and we will come to them and make our home with them." (John 14:23)

Jesus places Himself on the same level as the Father, claiming the same divine ability to dwell with believers everywhere.

Thus, even in the same chapter where Jesus says, *"My Father is greater than I,"* He also affirms His divine equality.

The fuller picture emerges in John 17:5:

"And now, Father, glorify me in your presence with the glory I had with you before the world began."

Before the incarnation, Jesus shared the Father's eternal glory. But when He became man, He humbled Himself, laying aside the outward display of His glory (Philippians 2:6–8). Therefore, when Jesus said, *"My Father is greater than I,"* He was referring to His earthly state of humility, not to an inferior nature. After His resurrection and ascension, that glory was fully restored.

This was not a denial of equality in essence, but a recognition of His temporary subordination in role during His mission on earth.

It is notable that Muslims often cite this verse to deny Jesus' deity. Yet in the same passage Jesus repeatedly calls God "My Father," a relationship the Qur'an explicitly rejects (Qur'an 6:101; 9:30; 19:88–93). Thus, the very verse appealed to actually affirms Jesus' unique divine sonship and, when read in context, His equality in essence with the Father.

So, to conclude, when Jesus said, *"My Father is greater than I,"* He was speaking of His temporary earthly humility, not of an inferior divine nature. After His return to heaven, His eternal glory was restored.

Therefore, John 14:28 does not deny Jesus' deity—it helps explain it.

Question 30

"The argument that Jesus is God because He raised people from the dead is false," some Muslims argue. "Have not other prophets also raised the dead?"

Answer

The Gospels record three occasions where Jesus raised the dead:

1. A young girl who had just died and was still in her bed (Mark 5:35–43).

2. A young man being carried to his burial place (Luke 7:11–15).

3. Lazarus, a man who had been dead and buried for four days (John 11:1–44).

1. Jairus' Daughter (Mark 5:35–43)

"Jesus entered the home of Jairus, a synagogue leader, where mourners were weeping loudly. He said, "The child is not dead but asleep." They laughed at Him. Then Jesus took her by the hand and commanded, "Talitha koum! (Little girl, I say to you, get up!)." Immediately, she rose and began to walk."

2. The Widow's Son at Nain (Luke 7:11–15)

As a funeral procession passed, Jesus' heart went out to the grieving widow. He touched the bier and said, *"Young man, I say to you, get up!"* The dead man sat up and began to speak, and Jesus gave him back to his mother.

3. Lazarus—Four Days in the Tomb (John 11:21–44)

Before raising Lazarus, Jesus declared:

"I am the resurrection and the life. The one who believes in me will live, even though they die." (John 11:25–26)

Then, standing at the tomb, He cried out in a loud voice: *"Lazarus, come out!"* The dead man came out, still wrapped in his grave clothes.

Notice How Jesus Raised the Dead

- By His own command: *"I say to you, get up!"*
- By describing death as mere sleep: (Mark 5:39; John 11:11)
- By teaching that all the dead will one day hear His voice:

"A time is coming when all who are in their graves will hear his voice and come out ..." (John 5:28–29)

This goes far beyond restoring physical life. Jesus promised resurrection to eternal life:

"For my Father's will is that everyone who looks to the Son and believes in him shall have eternal life, and I will raise them up at the last day." (John 6:40)

No prophet ever made such a claim.

How Jesus' Miracles Differ from Those of the Prophets?

- Elijah raised a boy by crying out to the Lord and stretching himself over the child (1 Kings 17:19–22).
- Elisha revived a boy after praying to God and lying on him twice until he came to life (2 Kings 4:32–35).
- Peter raised Tabitha, but only after kneeling down and praying first, seeking God's intervention (Acts 9:40–41).

In each case, the prophet prayed and waited for God to act. By contrast, Jesus raised the dead by His own authority, simply by speaking the command.

Furthermore, Jesus delegated power to His disciples to heal and perform miracles in His name (Matthew 10:1). Their power was derivative; His authority was intrinsic and absolute.

Jesus' Own Resurrection

Above all, Jesus Himself rose from the dead.

Peter testified:

"But God raised him from the dead, freeing him from the agony of death, because it was impossible for death to keep its hold on him." (Acts 2:24)

And again:

"You killed the author of life, but God raised him from the dead." (Acts 3:15)

Death could not hold Him because He is the Lord of life.

So, to conclude, Elijah, Elisha, and Peter raised the dead, but always through prayer and complete dependence on God.

Jesus, by contrast, raised the dead by His own word, promised resurrection to eternal life, and proved His divine nature by rising from the dead Himself.

Only God can give life.

Jesus demonstrated that He is God—by His words, His works, and His victory over death itself.

ANSWERS TO QUESTIONS

Question 31

How could the Gospels be trusted when Jesus spoke Aramaic, while the Gospels were written in Greek?

Answer

This question reflects a lack of familiarity with the culture and languages used in Israel during the time of Jesus.

While Jesus primarily spoke Aramaic, there is strong evidence that He also spoke Greek, the international language of the Roman Empire, which included Judea. In regions such as Galilee and Jerusalem, people were commonly bilingual or even trilingual, speaking Aramaic, Hebrew, and Greek. For instance, the Greeks who sought to speak with Jesus approached Philip, one of His disciples, with a Greek name, Phillip (John 12:21–22), indicating that communication in Greek was possible.

Jesus likely used Aramaic in intimate settings, but in public teaching or when conversing with Romans and Greeks, He probably spoke Greek as well. On the cross, Jesus spoke Aramaic—*"Eloi, Eloi, lama sabachthani"* (Matthew 27:46; Mark 15:34)—but He certainly used Greek in His interactions with the Roman centurion (Matthew 8:5–13) and with Pontius Pilate (John 18:33–38). The sign placed over Jesus' head during the crucifixion was written in Aramaic, Greek, and Hebrew, confirming the multilingual setting of that time (John 19:19–20).

The Gospel writers translated Jesus' teachings into Greek for their readers, just as a modern preacher might translate a sermon for a wider audience. Translation was not considered a distortion of meaning but a faithful transmission of truth. In fact, Jewish scholars had already translated the Hebrew Scriptures into Greek centuries earlier—the Septuagint (c. 250 B.C.).

Notably, the Gospels preserve Aramaic expressions that Jesus used, such as *"Talitha koum"* (*"Little girl, arise"*) (Mark 5:41) and *"Eloi, Eloi, lama sabachthani"* ("My God, my God, why have you forsaken me?") (Mark 15:34). These details demonstrate the writers' closeness to the original events and their care in preserving Jesus' actual words.

Furthermore, the earliest Christians were either eyewitnesses or in direct contact with eyewitnesses.

- Matthew was one of the Twelve disciples.
- John was an apostle and an eyewitness.
- Mark was a close companion of Peter.
- Luke was a companion of Paul.

Early Church Fathers such as Papias (d. 135) and Irenaeus (d. 202) confirmed that the Gospels were based on firsthand accounts.[1] Jewish oral tradition was renowned for its precision—disciples memorized their teacher's words with great care and accuracy.

Moreover, translation does not undermine reliability. Historians do not dismiss ancient works simply because they were written in a language different from that of the events described. For example, most of what we know about Socrates comes from Plato, though Socrates spoke a different dialect of Greek. Likewise, no one questions the historical accuracy of accounts about Alexander the Great, even though many were written in other languages long after his death. Compared with these, the Gospels were recorded much closer in time to the events they describe.

Finally, since this question is often raised by Muslims, it is worth noting that even the Qur'an affirms the trustworthiness of the Gospel:

"*He sent down the Torah and the Gospel.*" (Qur'an 3:3)

"*We sent Jesus, son of Mary, confirming the Torah before him, and We gave him the Gospel, wherein is guidance and light.*" (Qur'an 5:46–47)

So, to conclude, the fact that Jesus spoke Aramaic while the Gospels were written in Greek does not diminish their reliability. The writers were close to the events, translation was both natural and faithful, and the New Testament preserves not only the message but even some of Jesus' exact words—testifying to its authenticity and accuracy.

---

[1] Manders, J. D., "*Irenaeus and the Proof of the Gospel*", Huntsville Theological Institute, December 2nd, 2024

Question 32

How can you worship a God hanging on the cross—weak, helpless, and powerless?

Answer

Muslims who ask this question often overlook—or intentionally ignore—the message and ministry of the Cross.

Firstly, Jesus had complete authority over His own life. He said:

"No one takes my life from me, but I lay it down of my own accord.

I have authority to lay it down and authority to take it up again."

(John 10:18)

That is why, at the moment of His death, *"He bowed His head and gave up His spirit."* (John 19:30)

Before going up to Jerusalem, where He would be crucified, Jesus foretold in detail—seven times—what was going to happen to Him:

"Now Jesus was going up to Jerusalem. On the way, He took the Twelve aside and said to them, 'We are going up to Jerusalem, and the Son of Man will be delivered over to the chief priests and the teachers of the law. They will condemn Him to death and will hand Him over to the Gentiles to be mocked and flogged and crucified. On the third day, He will be raised to life." (Matthew 20:17–19; see also Matthew 16:21–23; Mark 8:31; 9:31–32; 10:33–34; Luke 9:22; 18:31–33)

In just these few verses, Jesus revealed:

- The place of His death — Jerusalem;
- The manner of His death — crucifixion;

- The timing of His resurrection — on the third day;
- The identity of those who would condemn Him — the Jewish leaders, and
- The agents who would carry out the sentence — the Gentiles (Romans).

Jesus also determined the exact day of His death. He avoided three previous attempts on His life by the Jews (John 5:16; 8:59; 11:53–54). But when the appointed time came—the Jewish Passover—He willingly surrendered Himself to the Roman authorities (John 18:7–8). He was crucified and died on Passover, because He Himself is our Passover Lamb (1 Corinthians 5:7).

When the Roman governor, Pontius Pilate, boasted of his power over Jesus—

"Don't you realize I have power either to free you or to crucify you?" (John 19:10)

Jesus replied,

"You would have no power over me if it were not given to you from above." (John 19:11)

When Peter, one of Jesus' disciples, tried to defend him with his sword, Jesus rebuked him:

"Put your sword back in its place," Jesus said to him, *"for all who draw the sword will die by the sword. Do you think I cannot call on my Father, and He will at once put at my disposal more than twelve legions of angels? But how then would the Scriptures be fulfilled that say it must happen in this way?"*

(Matthew 26:52–54; John 18:10)

So, to conclude, Jesus was not weak or helpless on the Cross. He was fully aware of, and in full control over, every event leading to His death and resurrection. His crucifixion was not a defeat but a divine act of love and authority. Jesus was never powerless—not even for a moment.

Question 33

The Gospel writers are anonymous—who are they? Who knows them? Were they really contemporary with Jesus?

Answer

The Gospels are formally anonymous in the same way most ancient works are—the author is not identified within the body of the text.

In modern literature, authorship is typically shown on the cover or title page. Critics, however, argue that the four Gospels were originally anonymous and that the names later attached to them—Matthew, Mark, Luke, and John—were added to enhance their authority.

Historical evidence and early Church testimony, however, refute this claim. Scholar Martin Hengel[1] observes that the Gospel titles ("According to Matthew," "According to Mark," etc.) were added before the end of the first century to distinguish them as they circulated more widely. By the mid–second century, these names were universally recognized and consistently associated with their respective Gospels.

For the purpose of comparison, the authorship of the Epistle to the Hebrews has been debated since ancient times, yet no such debate ever arose concerning the four canonical Gospels.

Renowned scholar Craig Evans[2] also notes that every surviving Gospel manuscript bears the name of its traditional author—with no competing attributions.

In his writings, Papias of Hierapolis[3], a second-century bishop and early Christian author, testifies that Mark, having been an interpreter of Apostle Peter, accurately recorded Peter's teachings. Papias also states that Matthew composed his Gospel in Hebrew, or Aramaic, preserving many of the sayings of Jesus.

The early Christian apologist Justin Martyr[4], writing around A.D. 150, referred to the Gospels as "the Memoirs of the Apostles and their Companions." His student, Tatian the Assyrian, later harmonized the four Gospels into a single work known as the *Diatessaron* ("Through Four") around A.D. 170–175.

Luke, a physician and companion of the Apostle Paul, dedicated his Gospel to *"Most Excellent Theophilus"* (Luke 1:3), who was likely a high-ranking Gentile believer personally known to Luke. Appropriately, Luke's Gospel includes more accounts of healing than any other—fitting for a physician (Colossians 4:14).

Matthew, a former tax collector—despised by the Jews as a collaborator with Rome—nevertheless gives his own name to one of the Gospels. It is also noteworthy that Matthew refers to money and taxes more frequently than the other evangelists.

Clement of Alexandria (A.D. 150–215), one of the great early Christian theologians, affirmed that Mark wrote down Peter's teachings and that Luke was closely associated with Paul.[5]

Polycarp[6], a disciple of Apostle John, was instructed by the Apostles themselves and later appointed as bishop of Smyrna. His own disciple, Irenaeus (A.D. 125–202), explicitly confirmed that the Gospel of Matthew was written by Matthew, that of Mark by Mark, that of Luke by Luke, and that of John by John.[7]

If, as some critics argue, the names of the Gospel writers were added in the second century to lend credibility, it would have been far more advantageous to attribute Mark's Gospel directly to Peter or Luke's to Paul—both far more prominent figures. Yet the early Church did not do so. This consistency strongly supports the authenticity of the traditional authorship.

So, to conclude, historical consistency, early manuscript evidence, and the testimony of the early Church collectively confirm—beyond reasonable doubt—that the four canonical Gospels were written by:

- Matthew, also known as Levi the son of Alphaeus in Mark 2:14 amnd Luke 5:27, the former tax collector and disciple of Jesus
- Mark, the companion of Apostle Peter. He is also known as John Mark as in Acts 12:12, 12:25, 13:5, 13:13; and Colossians 4:10.
- Luke, the beloved physician and companion of Paul as in Colossians 4:14. He is also mentioned in Philemon 24 and 2 Timothy 4:11
- John, the son of Zebedee, and Salome, brother of James. Jesus gave John and James the nickname "Sons of thunder." He is the disciple that Jesus loved (John 13:23; 19:26; 20:2; 21:7,20). He was an eyewitness disciple of Jesus Christ.

---

[1] Hengel, M. *The Four Gospels and the One Gospel of Jesus Christ: An Investigation into the Collection and Origin of the Canonical Gospels.* Trinity Press International, USA, 2000.

[2] Evans, C. *Fabricating Jesus: How Modern Scholars Distort the Gospels.* InterVarsity Press, USA, 2008.

[3] Papias fragments in *Christian Writings – Papias Fragments*, *Early Christian Writings – Papias*, and *Catholic Culture – Papias Fragments*.

[4] Justin Martyr, *The First Apology*, addressed to Roman authorities, c. A.D. 150.

[5] Clement of Alexandria, *Hypotyposes*, quoted in Eusebius, *Church History* 6.14.5–7 Luke as Paul's companion, Clement of Alexandria, quoted in Eusebius, *Church History* 5.8.4

[6] Eusebius, *Ecclesiastical History* 4.14.3.

[7] Irenaeus, *Against Heresies (Adversus Haereses)*, Book 3, Chapter 1, Paragraph 1.

Question 34

Why did Jesus cry out to God, saying, "My God, my God, why have you forsaken me" in Mark 15:34? How could God, according to Christian belief, cry out to "His God"? And how could God forsake Jesus?

Answer

This question refers to Matthew 27:45–46, which states:

"From noon until three in the afternoon, darkness came over all the land. About three in the afternoon, Jesus cried out in a loud voice, 'Eli, Eli, lema sabachthani?' (which means, 'My God, my God, why have you forsaken me.?")

This inquiry arises from the account in Matthew 27:45–46. At face value, the words 'My God, my God, why have you forsaken me?' might suggest a breakdown in the relationship between Father and Son. Yet, when we examine the language, context, and theological framework more carefully, a different picture emerges.

The biblical witness affirms that the Father remained with the Son. As Jesus says in John 8:29: '*My Father is with me; he has not left me alone, because I always do the things that please him.*' This statement underlines that the notion of an abandoned Son is not supported by Scripture as a whole.

There are two common objections to this passage.

1. The objection concerning Jesus' divinity

One common objection holds that because Jesus called the Father '*My God,*' He cannot himself be divine. However, this overlooks the doctrine of the Incarnation: the eternal Word became flesh in order that the divine might truly live within human existence.

In Jeremiah 32:27, God declares, "*I am the God of all flesh.*" Within Trinitarian theology, the eternal Word—who "was with God" and "was God" (John 1:1)—became incarnate in human flesh (John 1:14). As such, it is entirely appropriate that, in His humanity, Christ should address the Father as "My God." His words express His full participation in human experience and His submission to the Father's redemptive will—not a denial of His divine nature.

2. The objection concerning divine abandonment

Another challenge arises from how God could seemingly abandon His only-begotten Son. The three Synoptic Gospels describe darkness enveloping the land just before Jesus utters his cry (Matthew 27:45; Mark 15:33; Luke 23:44). Many interpreters see this blackness not just as a natural phenomenon but as the weight of divine judgment being placed on the sinless one who takes humanity's guilt upon himself.

At the ninth hour (3:00 p.m.), as Jesus uttered His cry, the darkness lifted. Far from being a cry of despair, His words reveal His deep awareness of the gravity of His mission: the fulfillment of Scripture and the completion of atonement. The removal of darkness immediately after His cry signifies divine response and vindication—the Father's acknowledgment that redemption had been accomplished, justice satisfied, and wrath appeased.

To understand Jesus' words more fully, we must turn to their Scriptural source. Jesus' cry on the cross directly quotes Psalm 22:1:

"*My God, my God, why have you forsaken me?*"

Psalm 22 is a Messianic psalm that vividly portrays the Messiah's suffering and ultimate vindication. While it begins with a lament of apparent abandonment, it concludes with a declaration of God's faithfulness toward the afflicted one:

"For he has not despised or scorned the suffering of the afflicted one; he has not hidden his face from him but has listened to his cry for help.", where "he" refers to Yahweh God, (Psalm 22:24).

Who is "the afflicted one" in Psalm 22, the one from whom Yahweh God has not hidden his face, but listened to his cry for help?

Psalm 22 leaves no doubt that Jesus Christ is the One being described and meant, as it contains striking prophetic parallels to the crucifixion:

- Verse 16: *"They pierce my hands and my feet"* — remarkably precise, considering crucifixion was unknown in the time of David, the Psalm writer (fulfilled in John 20:25, 27; Luke 24:39-40)
- Verse 18: *"They divide my clothes among them and cast lots for my garment"* (fulfilled in John 19:23–24).
- Verses 6–8: *"All who see me mock me… 'He trusts in the Lord,' they say, 'let the Lord rescue him'"*, echoed almost verbatim in Matthew 27:39–43.

Through these parallels, it becomes evident that Jesus intentionally cited Psalm 22 to identify Himself as its fulfillment. His suffering was neither accidental nor meaningless, but divinely ordained.

Therefore, Jesus' cry should be understood in this light. Rather than expressing despair—*"My God, my God, why have you forsaken me?"*—it can also be understood as an appeal within the redemptive process: "My God, my God, how long will You seem to forsake me?" If Jesus is the "afflicted one" of Psalm 22, which He clearly is, then the "forsaking" was temporary—lasting only until He completed the work the Father gave Him to do.

To grasp the deeper reason behind His cry, we must also recall the events in the Garden of Gethsemane, where Jesus prayed:

"My Father, if it is possible, may this cup be taken from me. Yet not as I will, but as you will." (Matt. 26:39)

The "cup" represents divine wrath and judgment against sin (cf. Isa. 51:17; Jer. 25:15). As the sinless substitute, Christ bore that wrath on behalf of humanity. His cry of "forsakenness" thus expresses the experience of bearing sin's penalty, not an actual separation within the Trinity.

Immediately after His cry, the Gospels record:

"Jesus gave up his spirit." (Matt. 27:50; cf. Mark 15:37; Luke 23:46; John 19:30)

This signifies not defeat, but the completion of His redemptive work and the voluntary surrender of His life into the Father's hands.

So, to conclude, Jesus' cry, "My God, my God, why have you forsaken me?" should not be regarded as a literal abandonment by God but as a profound theological declaration of His substitutionary suffering. It reveals that Christ, in His humanity, experienced the full weight of sin's alienation—yet remained perfectly obedient and trusting in the Father's will.

Psalm 22 moves from lament to triumph, from suffering to vindication. Likewise, Jesus' cry anticipates the resurrection, where divine approval and victory over sin and death were fully manifested.

When read in its full literary and theological context, this passage affirms, rather than undermines, the deity of Christ. It illustrates how selective or decontextualized readings can lead to misinterpretations—especially when the Christological and redemptive purposes of Scripture are overlooked.

Question 35

Some Muslims argue that Jesus did not claim exclusive divinity, suggesting He acknowledged the existence of other "gods" when He quoted Psalm 82 in His response to Jewish critics:

"Jesus answered them, 'Is it not written in your Law, "I have said you are 'gods'"? (John 10:34)

Context in John 10

In John 10, Jesus cites Psalm 82:6, repeating the phrase *"You are gods."* This exchange occurs during the Festival of Dedication (Hanukkah), when Jewish leaders pressed Him to declare clearly whether He was the Messiah:

"The Jews who were there gathered around him, saying, 'How long will you keep us in suspense? If you are the Messiah, tell us plainly.'" (John 10:24)

Jesus points to His works as evidence of His messianic identity, and then asserts His unity with God:

"I and the Father are one." (John 10:30)

This claim led the Jews to attempt to stone Him for blasphemy (John 10:31–33). In response, Jesus cites Psalm 82:6:

"Is it not written in your Law, 'I have said you are "gods"'? If he called them 'gods,' to whom the word of God came—and Scripture cannot be set aside—what about the one whom the Father set apart as his very own and sent into the world?" (John 10:34–36)

Understanding "gods" in Psalm 82

The Hebrew word translated "gods" is *elohim*. While most often used for the one true God, it can refer to other beings depending on context:

- Spiritual beings such as angels (Job 1:6; 38:7)
- Idols or false gods (Genesis 35:4; Deuteronomy 32:17)
- Human judges or rulers exercising authority on God's behalf (Exodus 21:6; 22:8–9; 28)

Psalm 82:1 mentions God presiding "in the great assembly," giving judgment among the "gods." Scholars generally offer two main interpretations:

1. Supernatural beings under God's authority

Here, the "gods" are understood as spiritual beings with delegated authority. God rebukes them for failing to judge justly and warns that they will *"die like mere mortals"* (Psalm 82:6–7). This interpretation aligns with passages about divine judgment on rebellious angels (Matthew 25:41; 2 Peter 2:4).

2. Human judges and rulers

Alternatively, the psalm addresses earthly leaders who act as God's representatives. Though called "gods" because of their authority, they remain mortal and accountable for corrupt actions:

"I said, 'You are gods; you are all sons of the Most High.' But you will die like mere men; you will fall like every other ruler." (Psalm 82:6–7)

Calling human rulers "gods" highlights their responsibility, their delegated power, and the fact that ultimate authority belongs to God (Psalm 82:8).

Jesus' Use of Psalm 82

When Jesus quotes Psalm 82:6, He refers to *"those to whom the word of God came"* (John 10:35), meaning those who received divine instruction or authority. His critics accused Him of blasphemy for claiming equality with God. In response, Jesus points out: if mortal judges can metaphorically be called "gods," then it is entirely appropriate for Him—the uniquely consecrated Son of God—to claim this title.

His argument does not suggest that humans are truly divine or that multiple gods exist. Rather, He highlights the inconsistency of His accusers, demonstrating that His claim to Sonship aligns with Scripture and surpasses the metaphorical application of the title to human judges.

The Jewish audience clearly grasped the significance: they recognized that Jesus was asserting true deity. This is why the attempt to seize Him continued (John 10:39). By citing Psalm 82, Jesus affirmed that He alone is the unique, divine Son of God—sanctified and sent by the Father—not merely one among many "gods," but the one who shares the Father's nature in fullness.

So, to conclude, Jesus in John 10:34, rather than numbering himself among other "gods", he made it so clear that he is the one and only true divine Son of God.

Question 36

How many lords do you have, Christians?"—Some Muslims ask, quoting Matthew 22:41–45:

"While the Pharisees were gathered, Jesus asked them, 'What do you think about the Messiah? Whose Son is he?' 'The son of David,' they replied... No one could say a word in reply, and from that day on no one dared to ask him any more questions."

Answer

First, Scripture clearly affirms that both Judaism and Christianity are monotheistic faiths. They believe in one Lord and one God. Deuteronomy 6:4 declares: "Hear, O Israel: The Lord our God, the Lord is one."

Almost 1,500 years later, Jesus Himself confirmed the very same truth when asked about the greatest commandment (Mark 12:29).

In the passage Muslims cite, Matthew 22:41–45, Jesus initiates a discussion with the Pharisees, the religious elite of Israel who knew the Hebrew Scriptures well. Jesus asks them: "Whose son is the Messiah?"

The Jews answered immediately: "The son of David."

They believed, based on their Scriptures, that the Messiah would be a descendant of David. Isaiah had prophesied about 700 years earlier:

"A shoot will come up from the stump of Jesse; from his roots a Branch will bear fruit. The Spirit of the Lord will rest on him..." (Isaiah 11:1–2)

Jesse was the father of King David.

Jeremiah further clarified that this promised "Branch" was a royal descendant of David:

"I will raise up for David a righteous Branch, a King who will reign wisely... This is the name by which he will be called: The Lord Our Righteous Savior." (Jeremiah 23:5–6)

Thus, the Pharisees were correct: the Messiah would be David's son.

But Jesus then asked a second question—one they could not answer:

"How is it then that David, speaking by the Spirit, calls him 'Lord'? For he says: 'The LORD said to my Lord: Sit at my right hand until I put your enemies under your feet.' If then David calls him 'Lord,' how can he be his son?"

Jesus was quoting Psalm 110:1, a psalm well known to the Pharisees:

"The LORD says to my Lord: 'Sit at my right hand until I make your enemies a footstool for your feet.'"

This psalm was written by David around 1000 B.C.

David, a devout monotheistic Jew, believed there was one LORD—Yahweh. Yet he spoke of two figures, both bearing divine titles.

So how do we understand this?

In Hebrew, the distinction becomes clear:

- "The LORD" = יהוה (Yahweh) — the divine name of God.
- "my Lord" = לָאדֹנִי (Adonai) — a title of honour and divine authority, often used for God Himself.

In the Hebrew Bible, *Adonai* is sometimes used interchangeably with Yahweh (e.g., Isaiah 50:4; Psalm 2:7; Psalm 110:4).

Psalm 110:1 also describes this second "Lord" as sitting at the right hand of Yahweh, ruling until His enemies are subdued. This allows us to identify Him: Scripture repeatedly teaches that Jesus Christ is the One seated at God's right hand:

- Matthew 26:64 – "You will see the Son of Man sitting at the right hand of the Mighty One…"
- Mark 14:62 – "You will see the Son of Man sitting at the right hand of the Mighty One…"
- Luke 22:69 – "The Son of Man will be seated at the right hand of the mighty God."
- Acts 2:33–34 – Peter: "Exalted to the right hand of God…"
- Acts 7:56 – Stephen: "I see the Son of Man standing at the right hand of God."

David, by the Spirit, saw the Messiah—a thousand years before Christ's incarnation—exalted at Yahweh's right hand.

The Pharisees were unable to answer Jesus because they misunderstood the true identity of the Messiah standing before them. Jesus later removed all doubt when He declared:

"I am the Root and the Offspring of David." (Revelation 22:16)

So, to conclude, there are not two gods or two competing "lords" in Matthew 22:41–45.

There is:

1. Yahweh, the one God of Israel
2. The Messiah, the incarnate Word of Yahweh—Jesus Christ—whom David calls "my Lord" and whom Scripture identifies as seated at God's right hand

Christian monotheism remains intact. The passage reinforces, rather than challenges, the identity of Jesus as the divine Messiah foretold in the Old Testament and revealed in the New.

About The Author

Dr. Yousry Sidrak has been studying Islam and engaging with Muslims for over 20 years. He holds a PhD in Chemical Engineering, a Diploma in Christian Divinity, and an MSc in Islamic Studies from the Centre of Excellence in Islamic Studies at the University of Melbourne, Australia. Dr. Sidrak lived in Muslim-majority countries for more than 40 years, including serving as a Professor of Chemical Engineering at King Fahd University of Petroleum and Minerals in Saudi Arabia—the birthplace of Islam. He currently delivers seminars on how to use the Qur'an to introduce Jesus to Muslims, writes and publishes articles on building bridges between Christianity and Islam, and has supervised PhD students in Islamic studies. He has published over 30 articles in international journals, including those focused on Islamic theology and philosophy.

Dr. Sidrak's passion is to teach Christians about Islam and to introduce Jesus to Muslims.